"Brian O'Leary conceived his book a 'landscape' of Ignatian spirituality— and context and its current experience in a very different context. The 'landscape' most readers think familiar, in this writer's hands turns out to be full of rich surprises. *God Ever Greater* is a book to hold on to."

    —Joseph A. Tetlow, SJ
      Director of Montserrat Jesuit Retreat House
      Lake Dallas, Texas

"Like Ignatius, O'Leary 'begins' where we are, and then progressively helps us to move more deeply so that we can both better understand and respond more generously to a God who is always greater."

    —James T. Bretzke, SJ
      Professor of Theology
      John Carroll University

# God Ever Greater

*Exploring Ignatian Spirituality*

Brian O'Leary, SJ

**LITURGICAL PRESS**

Collegeville, Minnesota

www.litpress.org

Cover design by Monica Bokinskie. Image courtesy of Wikimedia Commons. *The Vision of Ignatius of Loyola*, ca. 1622–1630, oil on canvas.

First published in 2018 by Messenger Publications. © Brian O'Leary, SJ, 2019. This edition of *God Ever Greater* is published by arrangement with Messenger Publications, Dublin, Ireland.

Published by Liturgical Press, Collegeville, Minnesota. All rights reserved. No part of this book may be used or reproduced in any manner whatsoever, except brief quotations in reviews, without written permission of Liturgical Press, Saint John's Abbey, PO Box 7500, Collegeville, MN 56321-7500. Printed in the United States of America.

| 1 | 2 | 3 | 4 | 5 | 6 | 7 | 8 | 9 |
| --- | --- | --- | --- | --- | --- | --- | --- | --- |

**Library of Congress Cataloging-in-Publication Data**

Names: O'Leary, Brian, author.
Title: God ever greater : exploring Ignatian spirituality / Brian O'Leary, SJ.
Description: Collegeville, Minnesota : Liturgical Press, 2020. | Summary: "Provides an introduction to Ignatian spirituality"— Provided by publisher.
Identifiers: LCCN 2020023270 (print) | LCCN 2020023271 (ebook) | ISBN 9780814688137 (paperback) | ISBN 9780814688373 (epub) | ISBN 9780814688373 (mobi) | ISBN 9780814688373 (pdf)
Subjects: LCSH: Ignatius, of Loyola, Saint, 1491-1556. | Spirituality—Catholic Church.
Classification: LCC BX2350.65 .O49 2020 (print) | LCC BX2350.65 (ebook) | DDC 248—dc23
LC record available at https://lccn.loc.gov/2020023270
LC ebook record available at https://lccn.loc.gov/2020023271

# Contents

References   vii

Prologue   ix

**Part One**
**Towards an Understanding of Ignatian Spirituality**

1. What is Spirituality?   3

2. Ignatius: Life and Legacy   16

3. *Acta Patris Ignatii*: The Autobiography   32

4. Mystical Gifts   46

5. Discernment in the Tradition   61

6. Personal and Corporate   77

**Part Two**
**Towards a Personal Response to Ignatian Spirituality**

1. Ignatius the Pilgrim   95

2. Learning from Daydreams   99

3. Three Things I Pray   104

4. Light and Darkness   108

5. Freedom for Discernment   113

6. To the Greater Glory   117

7. The Call to Interiority   122

# References

The three most quoted works in this book are the Bible and two texts that go back to Ignatius himself, the *Spiritual Exercises* and the so-called *Autobiography*. For the sake of consistency I have used the following translations throughout.

*Holy Bible:* New Revised Standard Version. London: HarperCollins (1997).

The Scripture quotations contained herein are from the New Revised Standard Version, copyright © 1989, by the Division of Christian Education of the National Council of the Churches of Christ in the USA and are used by permission. All rights reserved.

*The Spiritual Exercises of Saint Ignatius.* A translation and commentary by George E. Ganss, SJ, Chicago: Loyola University Press (1992).

*A Pilgrim's Journey: The Autobiography of Ignatius of Loyola.* A translation and commentary by Joseph N. Tylenda, SJ, San Francisco: Ignatius Press (2001; revised edition).

Quotations from the *Exercises* and *Autobiography* (including its two prefaces) will be given the paragraph numbers that are now in universal use, e.g. [12].

# Prologue

Children love to explore. Whether it be a forest, a beach, a cave or an attic the cry of 'Let's explore!' signals the beginning of an adventure. They are in search of knowledge, certainly, but above all they seek the tingling sensation of entering the unknown and the excitement of discovery. Adults too can have this thirst for exploration. Indeed, without it, civilisations would ossify.

The lifespan of Ignatius Loyola coincides with the period of exploration that opened up the the Americas, as well as parts of Africa and Asia, to European sailors, soldiers, traders and missionaries. This was the start of a slow learning curve for Europeans, as they were forced over time to re-evaluate their place in the world. They could no longer automatically presume that they constituted the centre of the world, or believe that their cultures were normative. Of course it took centuries for Eurocentric thinking to die out completely – or almost completely. Fifteenth- and sixteenth-century explorations brought wealth in abundance pouring into Europe from these newly discovered regions, but they also brought art, music, philosophy and religious beliefs. Life in Europe, and in the wider world, could never be the same again. This was all because of the innate human instinct or passion for exploration.

My use of the word 'exploring' in the subtitle of this book is meant to awaken the reader's own personal urge to explore. Might it even elicit a like sense of anticipation? A tingling of excitement? Here the object of exploration is not a continent, or a remote wilderness, or a new trade route or the mysteries of outer space.

ix

x *God Ever Greater*

In this book I will be travelling through, observing, noting, attempting to discover the 'landscape' of Ignatian spirituality. This is the journey on which I invite you to accompany me.

Some readers may have visited here before, liked what they saw, and now want to return. They sense that there is more to see, more to learn, and further enrichment to be had. For others, Ignatian spirituality may be virgin territory, unexplored and therefore somewhat mysterious and even vaguely intimidating. I hope to guide beginners as well as the more experienced through this landscape, without the former being left behind, or the latter feeling that they should really have made this journey on their own. So let's explore.

A secondary reason for my use of the word 'exploring' is that I am not attempting a total coverage, still less a systematic presentation of Ignatian spirituality. The landscape is much too vast for a project of that kind. In fact, considering the extensive library of writings on Ignatian spirituality, no author has succeeded in presenting it in its totality. So I shall be offering something more manageable, approaching the subject from different angles and different starting points, and exploring the terrain that I encounter. And like the famous explorers of Ignatius's lifetime, I would hope to end my investigations with further unanswered questions swirling around in my readers' minds, questions to mull over, maybe even to bring to prayer. A final word of wisdom from T. S. Eliot:

> We shall not cease from exploration
> And the end of all our exploring
> Will be to arrive where we started
> And know the place for the first time.[1]

## Structure and Content

The book has two parts. The first and longer part is explanatory and discursive. It makes use of history, including the writings of

---

1. T.S. Eliot, 'Little Gidding' (from *Four Quartets*). London: Faber and Faber (ninth impression, 1976).

Ignatius and other early Jesuits, and theology, insofar as it is relevant to the task. These chapters are meant to lead to an understanding of the matters being presented. They will not use academic language, however, and whenever technical words cannot be avoided, they will be explained in clear terms. The aim is comprehension, not obfuscation!

## Part I

Chapter 1 is, in many ways, foundational for what is to follow. Instead of beginning with Ignatius or with specifically Ignatian topics, I raise the question, 'What is spirituality?' A vagueness about the answer is widespread and can lead people astray. It is better to make sure that we grasp the meaning of the noun, 'spirituality', before examining the adjective, 'Ignatian'.

Chapter 2 introduces the life of Ignatius, presented here in outline. Ignatian spirituality was not based on some pre-existing theory but grew out of the lived experiences of this man, who was rooted in a particular historical and cultural context. We also need some familiarity with Ignatius's personality and how this developed over a lifetime. During his conversion, Ignatius came to realise that all was gift from God, and he later recognised that God was calling him to share what he had received with others. To do this, the chief means he chose – or, more correctly, was given – were the Spiritual Exercises. These became his legacy to us and it is fitting that we introduce them here.

Chapter 3 continues to reflect on Ignatius's life, but now as viewed through the lens of his so-called *Autobiography*. This book is frequently put into the hands of those enquiring about Ignatian spirituality, and with good reason. It is regarded as a helpful introduction and is easy reading. A second or third perusing of the text, however, will show that it is actually quite an enigmatic little book that needs to be scrutinised carefully. Some background to its composition can be helpful in enabling the reader to profit from it.

Chapter 4 explores Ignatian mysticism. In current studies of Ignatius, this is one of the areas that is receiving the most attention.

xii *God Ever Greater*

On a popular level also, it is his mystical gifts which most attract contemporary men and women to Ignatius and his legacy. Surprisingly, this is a new development as, for the first four hundred years after his death, his mystical gifts were either downplayed or ignored completely. But in today's cultural climate, where there is almost a cult of mysticism, often defined rather loosely, it is not surprising that interest in Ignatius's mysticism is strong.

Chapter 5 opens up the area of discernment. For many the term discernment is almost synonymous with Ignatian spirituality. Despite that perception, however, both the theory and practice of discernment have a much longer history in the Judeo-Christian tradition. Some knowledge of this tradition will help us to see how Ignatius learned from those who went before him, and ask what he may have contributed to expand that tradition. I will suggest that he was indeed innovative in showing how the discernment of spirits could be used in the context of decision-making.

Chapter 6 enters another section of the landscape that has only lately received much attention. I refer to the corporate dimension of Ignatian spirituality. Far from being individualistic, as many have claimed, Ignatian spirituality has always had a corporate dimension. Without it, the Society of Jesus – better known as the Jesuits – could not have come to exist. But it was not recognised until recently how the spirituality of the Society, as articulated in its *Constitutions*, could be applicable to lay religious groups or even secular organisations. Much work has now been done showing that this is, in fact, possible. I will not explore this development in detail but will concentrate on a document called 'The Deliberation of the First Fathers'. This describes how Ignatius and his early companions reached their decision to become a religious order. It has become a template for any process of group decision-making in the Ignatian tradition.

## Part II

The second part of this book was originally a series of articles in the monthly magazine *The Sacred Heart Messenger*, published in Dublin by Messenger Publications. Here they are reworked and expanded a little. These articles take up some of the themes from Part I, but in a simpler and more experiential way. These short pieces are meant to be read slowly, preferably one at a time, and pondered over. One might call them meditations. They aim less at leading the reader to understanding, as in Part I, and more at awakening a personal response. They suggest how Ignatian spirituality can deepen and enrich the reader's relationship with the 'God Who is Ever Greater'.

Some readers, especially if they regard themselves as beginners, might do well to reverse the usual sequence in reading a book. This would involve engaging with Part II before starting Part I. Another possibility would be to intermingle articles from Part II with the chapters of Part I. Whatever helps most is good!

*Part One*

# Towards
# an Understanding
# of Ignatian Spirituality

*chapter one*

# What is Spirituality?

The human race has always been aware of the world of the spirit or of spirits. This world is approached with a mixture of trepidation and celebration. In Rudolf Otto's famous phrase it is experienced as the *mysterium tremendum et fascinans* – the mystery that makes us tremble in awe while, at the same time, powerfully attracting us to itself. This kind of awareness goes back to the dawn of human history, although the term 'spirituality' is of relatively recent origin. We will not find it in the Bible, or in the writings of the Fathers of the Church, or in medieval or Reformation-era theologians. The word only began to appear in the seventeenth century in French Catholic writing, and it was used as a synonym for the inner life. Seventeenth-century France was experiencing a Golden Age of mysticism, as Spain had in the sixteenth century. A fascination with the inner life was part of its religious culture, but it took more time for 'spirituality' to be accepted as a valid term in academic theology. Of late, however, it has replaced more established terms such as 'ascetical theology', 'mystical theology' or 'theology of the spiritual life'. Departments of spirituality now exist in many third-level institutions of learning.

## Non-religious Influences

At the same time a new phenomenon has surfaced: the adopting or the usurping – depending on your point of view – of the word

4  *Towards an Understanding of Ignatian Spirituality*

'spirituality' within the secular world. What until recently had been a specifically religious term, has now come to represent a range of human values, admirable in themselves but not explicitly arising from, or linked with, any faith tradition. For example, not only humanitarian organisations such as schools and hospitals, but many financial institutions, banks, multinationals and businesses of all kinds make use of the word 'spirituality' in their vision statements, making it part of their rhetoric. These corporations promote the development of 'spirituality' within their workforce. This will not require any faith-commitment, but anything that engenders a feel-good factor and harmonious relations in the workplace will be brought under its banner. 'Spirituality' is perceived as fostering the well-being and happiness of the women and men in the corporation's workforce. This goal is not entirely altruistic on the part of the employers, however. Their bottom line is that a happy workforce is a more productive workforce, and higher production rates ensure larger profits. Some might regard this use of 'spirituality' as a bit cynical; leaving that aside, however, this development does make the term itself more confusing, even ambiguous.

## Spiritual but Not Religious

In the western world we have grown accustomed to hearing the assertion, even by nominal Christians, that 'I am spiritual, but not religious'. This is a modern phenomenon that has been caused, or at least exacerbated, by the secularisation of society. Our ancestors, probably up to the period of the Enlightenment in the late seventeenth and eighteenth centuries, would not have been able to understand someone making this claim. A non-religious spirituality would have been regarded as a contradiction in terms in ancient and medieval times. The situation is evidently different today and this new phenomenon calls for investigation. We might begin by looking at three categories of people who make the 'spiritual but not religious' declaration.

The first and most obvious category is comprised of atheists and agnostics. These either deny the reality of God (atheists) or are convinced that, even if there is a God, his or her existence cannot be proved (agnostics). In either case the God question is irrelevant for all practical purposes. Human beings must get on with life without a God and must find meaning elsewhere. What is then proposed is some version of secular humanism. Within this frame of reference a non-religious, humanist or secular spirituality emerges.

A second category consists of those who believe in a personal God but see no need to belong to a faith community. Many never had any religious affiliation in the first place. They became aware of God, or at least of the world of spirit, through some significant life experience or accumulation of experiences. Some in this category, however, do come from a religious background, but for various reasons they have abandoned their religious affiliation and now regard themselves simply as spiritual.

In this sub-group there are those who make this choice on grounds that are, at least implicitly, theological. Others have been influenced by more personal issues. They may have suffered injustice, real or perceived, at the hand of their church, or synagogue, or temple. They may be disillusioned by the politicking of religious leaders or by the hair-splitting of professional theologians. They may have been shocked by those very real scandals of which all are painfully aware, even if they themselves are not survivors of abuse. In the Christian context they profess to be distancing themselves from the institutional Church but not necessarily from Christ or God. They may continue to pray, and even use elements of the Christian spiritual tradition that they find helpful and nourishing. Some may know and appreciate the Bible and the writings of the mystics better than many Church-affiliated Christians. These people have committed themselves to what is often called 'the spiritual journey' or 'the inner journey'. That is their understanding of spirituality and it does not involve any belonging to a community of faith.

A third category represents another recent phenomenon in human thought. For some people the latest science, based on quantum theory, and particularly the new cosmology that comes

6    *Towards an Understanding of Ignatian Spirituality*

with it, has brought them to a radical conclusion. They believe that all religions have been part of an earlier phase in the evolutionary progress of planet Earth, often interpreted as coinciding with the reign of patriarchy. In light of evolutionary developments, they proclaim the death of religion and, in its place, the emergence of an ecological, planetary and cosmic spirituality. They may still speak of God, but this God is so immanent in the cosmos as to be identical with the evolutionary process itself. There is a remarkable confluence here of a scientific worldview, eco-feminism and New Age religiosity. The result, which is monistic and pantheistic, leaves no place for a transcendent, personal God such as that of Christian revelation.

## Two Models of Spirituality

At this point it may be helpful to examine briefly two basic models of spirituality. Each has its own legitimacy and, as we shall see, each can benefit from the other. What distinguishes them is their different interpretations of spirit, the concept that lies at the core of spirituality.

### First Model: The Human Spirit

The first model understands the word 'spirit' to refer primarily, or even exclusively, to the human spirit. In this meaning spirit, and consequently spirituality, represents that dimension of the human person that makes us capable of self-transcendence. This capacity consists in the desire, freedom and determination to centre our lives, not on self-satisfaction or narrow self-interest, but on a value or values that lie outside of, or beyond, the self.

For example, the appreciation of beauty, in any or all of its forms, is liberating as well as uplifting. Beauty evokes, even beyond sensual pleasure, feelings of admiration, wonder, astonishment, praise and authentic joy. It enables us to transcend ourselves. Philosophers of beauty frequently use language shared with, and often borrowed from, spiritual writers, and especially mystical writers. They point out that the human response to beauty can lead to ecstasy or rapture. An aesthetic experience lifts us up, as it were, on to a higher plane, and enables us to exist, at least for that moment, outside of the self.

Another example is what we call humanitarianism. Our empathy with those who are suffering, and our willingness to help others even at a heavy cost to ourselves, also draw us into the world of transcendent values. We develop a radically different *Weltanschauung*, a new way of looking at the world. From this different global perspective, we find our horizons being enlarged and our vision sharpened. It is as if we are seeing everyone and everything with new eyes. Our priorities, so often unquestioned, are rearranged, with humane – or spiritual – values rising to the top. At the same time the scope of our inner freedom is expanded and we find within us a fresh energy and enthusiasm. This enables us to make decisions and to fashion our lives in the light of what we now see as authentic and worthwhile values. All this transformation is driven by the human spirit.

### Second Model: The Divine Spirit

A specifically Christian approach wants the primary meaning of spirit to be in reference to the Holy Spirit. We find this expressed in the letters of St Paul. People are spiritual, or are nurturing their spirituality, in so far as they are allowing the Holy Spirit to be more and more influential in their lives. Paul teaches that there is a spirit in God – the Holy Spirit – and there is also a spirit in each human person. First through creation, and then through baptism, a special relationship exists between the Spirit of God and the human spirit.

> When we cry 'Abba, Father' it is that very Spirit bearing witness with our spirit that we are children of God, and if children, then heirs, heirs of God and joint heirs with Christ (Rom 8:15-17).

The existence of a human spirit is crucial to Paul's teaching. In this he agrees with most humanists. He also believes, however, in the Holy Spirit, the Spirit of God, and that this Spirit too has been given to us, indeed dwells within us. Growth and maturity consist

8 *Towards an Understanding of Ignatian Spirituality*

in a gradual penetration of the human spirit by the Spirit of God. When that happens to a significant degree the person can be described as spiritual. We might say that what we call spirituality today is, for Paul, all that happens in the interaction between the Spirit of God and our human spirit. Spirituality in this sense is not simply my desire for, capacity for or efforts towards self-fulfilment or even self-transcendence. Spirituality is an interpersonal, mutual, dialogic relationship with God that takes place at the level of spirit – God's and ours. Within this relationship we are divinised, which for Christians is the ultimate transcendence.

## Reciprocal Models

This second model of spirituality, based on the pervasive action of the *divine spirit* as envisaged by Paul, need not be entirely in conflict with the first model which posits the *human spirit* alone. The latter model too has much to teach us. At the very least, it alerts us to the dynamics of the human spirit which are always in play and cannot be denied or disowned. It acts as a warning not to be too other-worldly in our approach to spirituality, downplaying human experience in order to preserve, or even exalt, the mystery of divine action in our lives. As the well-known scholastic adage assures us: grace builds on nature.

The first model reminds us to 'own' this human nature of ours, to pay attention to it, to be grateful for it and to develop its potential. It also prompts us to attend to the role of culture, its omnipresence and influence in our lives. It encourages us to take seriously whatever the dominant philosophy of the age may be, and it invites us to find good in, and esteem the values of, the secular world. Without an openness to the realities highlighted in the first model, our Christian spirituality runs the risk of descending into mere devotionalism. This can be defined as a religious sentimentality that ignores, not only reason and true human affectivity, but sound theology as well. In an extreme form it is a type of spiritual fundamentalism. Such is not the work of the Holy Spirit.

*What is Spirituality?* 9

## Culture

It may be helpful here to expand the reference to culture made above. The word 'culture' in this context does not mean in any exclusive sense the so-called 'high' culture that is focused on the creative arts. Culture, as here understood, is rather the way in which any group of people, large or small, live, think, feel, organise themselves, celebrate and share life. In every such culture there are underlying systems of values, meanings and views of the world, which are expressed publicly in language, gestures, symbols, rituals and manners. This is the broader meaning of culture that Paul VI was referring to when he said that 'the split between the gospel and culture is without a doubt the tragedy of our times'.[2] His successors have continued to point to this split as a dangerous reality with which Christians must grapple.

We have learned that, for better or for worse, we cannot distance ourselves from culture. It is all-pervasive. Its images bombard our senses. Its ideas fill our minds. Culture is like the air we breathe which may be healthy or polluted. Much of the time we are not conscious of its impact on us. Surreptitiously it is supplying us with most, or at least many, of our presuppositions – those beliefs and convictions that seem so innate in us that we rarely, if ever, think to question them. Culture is like a lens through which we look at the world. This lens may either illumine or distort reality, often in ways we may not realise.

Contemporary culture in the West, even though once shaped by Christian beliefs, now excludes *any* kind of religious faith from among its accepted values. Faith itself – whether Christian, Jewish, Islamic, Hindu or other – is frequently dismissed as infantile superstition that the human family needs to outgrow. It is also seen by many as a cause of social division, as illustrated by controversies around faith schools and other faith-based institutions. The dominant culture would prefer to have voices of faith excluded

2. Paul VI, *Evangelii Nuntiandi* (1975), 20.

10  *Towards an Understanding of Ignatian Spirituality*

from the public arena and the practice of faith become a purely private undertaking. For these and other reasons, people who embrace Christian spirituality as a way of life, do so in a cultural environment that is either hostile or indifferent to their values.

## Definitions of Christian Spirituality

Our next step will be to examine some working definitions of Christian spirituality proposed by three modern writers. Questions that you as reader might keep in mind include the following: Do these definitions strike you as being consistent with what we have been exploring up to now? Do they help to clarify anything that was obscure or do they raise new questions for you? Are they broader definitions than you might have expected or do you find them in any way restrictive? I will quote three working definitions supplied by Alister E. McGrath in his book *Christian Spirituality* – two of them from other writers, and the third his own.[3]

- Spirituality has to do with our experiencing of God and with the transformation of our consciousness and our lives as outcomes of that experience (Richard McBrien).

- [Spirituality] is a useful term to describe how, individually and collectively, we personally appropriate the traditional Christian beliefs about God, humanity and the world, and express them in terms of our basic attitudes, life-style and activity (Philip Sheldrake).

- Christian spirituality concerns the quest for a fulfilled and authentic Christian existence, involving the bringing together of the fundamental ideas of Christianity and the whole experience of living on the basis of and within the scope of the Christian faith (Alister E. McGrath).

3. Alister E. McGrath, *Christian Spirituality*. Oxford: Blackwell Publishing (1999), 3-4.13.

There is an obvious concurrence between these three definitions. Notice especially the holistic nature of spirituality as these authors see it. O'Brien emphasises 'the transformation of our consciousness and our lives'; Sheldrake stresses the need to express our faith 'in terms of our basic attitudes, life-style and activity'; and McGrath points to 'the quest for a fulfilled and authentic Christian existence'. There is no compartmentalisation involved here, no suggestion of some special part of ourselves that can be labelled as 'spiritual', or that has the capacity to become 'spiritual' in isolation from the whole. The human spirit is the spirit of the total person. It cannot be separated from that person's bodiliness, social make-up and insertion into the world.

Certainly we can speak of an inner journey, or of the need for interiority, or of the centrality of prayer, but this inner life has to express itself exteriorly – in our relationships, our choice of career, our leisuretime activities, even our politics. Each of us is one integrated person, and it is this person who is either spiritual or not, transformed or not, divinised or not. Any compartmentalisation would lead to dilettantism, inauthenticity and a denial of our humanity. We need to keep Christ's humanity before our eyes as our supreme model. The Incarnation has many implications for our spirituality.

Notice also how each writer, either implicitly or explicitly, presumes that the person living a Christian spirituality is part of a community of faith. This has many ramifications. Christian spirituality, of its very nature, is communal or corporate as well as personal. It is not just about the 'me', the self; and not even just about 'me and God'. It is not solipsistic. In the biblical creation story we read of God saying, 'It is not good that the man should be alone' (Gen 2:18). Indeed, as writers such as Martin Buber taught, an individual becomes fully a person only in relationship with other persons. We are social beings. This means that we are not solitary pilgrims on this earth but a community of pilgrims on a shared journey into the mystery that is God. We need each other for support and encouragement along the way. 'No man is

## 12   *Towards an Understanding of Ignatian Spirituality*

an island': John Donne's oft-quoted line admirably sums up this conviction. But it is to Paul we need to turn for the clearest presentation of the corporate nature of the Christian life, hence of Christian spirituality. He bases his argument on our essential oneness in the body of Christ.

> For just as the body is one and has many members, and all the members of the body, though many, are one body, so it is with Christ. . . . Indeed, the body does not consist of one member but of many. If the foot would say, 'Because I am not a hand, I do not belong to the body', that would not make it any less a part of the body. And if the ear would say, 'Because I am not an eye, I do not belong to the body', that would not make it any less a part of the body. If the whole body were an eye, where would the hearing be? If the whole body were hearing, where would the sense of smell be? But as it is, God arranged the members in the body, each one of them, as he chose. If all were a single member, where would the body be? As it is, there are many members, yet one body (1 Cor 12:12, 14-20).

### Luther on Faith and Works

There is an interesting parallel between this discussion on the nature of Christian spirituality and a central pillar of Martin Luther's theology. We have been advocating the need for a holistic approach to spirituality. The inner relationship that we are nurturing with God through prayer needs to be lived out in the world of people – family, friends and colleagues – and in the larger world of culture and politics. Spirituality has been pithily described as 'prayer elevated to a lifestyle'. Our prayer is meant to flow into every aspect of our lives, even the most banal. There is no boundary marking the place where life ends and prayer begins, or prayer ends and life begins. Prayer and life are one reality, and both are simultaneously personal and communal.

Apart from the dramatic scene of his nailing ninety-five theses to the door of the Castle Church in Wittenberg, Luther is perhaps best remembered for his theological position on justification. He

*What is Spirituality?* 13

held that it is attained by faith alone (*sola fide*) and not through the performance of good works. This became the central issue in his disputes with Catholic theologians during the Reformation. A master of rhetoric, Luther asserted this doctrine so passionately that his opponents were constantly accusing him of disparaging good works in the Christian life. Luther felt that he was being misinterpreted and insisted that he had no such intention. He made a number of efforts to clarify what he really meant. These are well represented in a number of passages in his 'Preface to the Epistle to the Romans', of which the following is an example:

> Faith is an unflappable confidence in God's grace, so certain that one would die a thousand deaths for it. This confidence and knowledge of God's grace that the Holy Spirit accomplishes through faith makes one happy, courageous and joyful before God and all creatures. Therefore, without constraint a person is willing and desires to do good to everyone and to serve everyone, to suffer all manner of things out of love and praise for God, who has revealed this grace. Therefore, it is impossible to separate works from faith, just as it is impossible to separate burning and light from fire.[4]

Luther lived before the word 'spirituality' had gained currency, yet this paragraph can be described as a powerful expression of Christian spirituality. Notice the primacy of the Holy Spirit, the centrality of faith and the way in which good works flow from faith. Works do not earn or even prepare us for justification, yet they inevitably flow from the experience of being justified. Luther is far from devaluing good works. On the contrary he wants them to flourish in the Christian life. His is not the only possible explanation of the relationship between faith and works – the Council of Trent was later to disagree with him – but it is, nevertheless, a persuasive

---

4. Martin Luther, 'Preface to the Epistle to the Romans', edited and translated by Philip D. W. Krey and Peter D. S. Krey, in *Luther's Spirituality*. New York/Mahwah: Paulist Press (2007), 109.

## 14  *Towards an Understanding of Ignatian Spirituality*

one. In particular, the final sentence in the quotation above provides us with a metaphor that lasts long in the imagination.

## The One and the Many

A not uncommon question asks, 'Is there one Christian spirituality or many?' The answer has to be nuanced: there is only *one* Christian spirituality, yet it expresses itself in a *multiplicity* of ways. Christians look to ground their spirituality in the Bible. Hence all Christian spirituality is biblical or evangelical. It is a lived response in faith to God's self-revelation in the Old and New Testaments. People, however, respond differently to what they read in these sacred writings. We might speak of a *resonance of the heart* that is unique to each person. The compilation of biblical stories, personalities, symbols, images and teachings resonates in a different way in one person than in another.

I may be so moved by the compassion that I see at work in the person and ministry of Jesus that compassion becomes the cornerstone of my spirituality. My whole life becomes an expression of the compassion that flows through me. It affects all my decision-making. You, on the other hand, may be captivated and challenged by the story of the rich young man. Because of this particular resonance you embrace a spirituality of radical simplicity. You model your life on that of the poor Jesus who 'emptied himself, taking the form of a slave' (Phil. 2:7). The fact that we have different responses to the gospel does not mean that either of us is living more authentically than the other. However, each of us is choosing – or has been chosen! – to live the *one* Christian spirituality in a particular way and with a distinctive emphasis.

Over the centuries certain specially gifted people have experienced God in such profound ways that others have looked to them for inspiration and encouragement. In their lifetime they were regarded as wisdom figures, models and exponents of the inner life. In some cases, and not always deliberately, they have become founders of a school of spirituality, or of a tradition that continued after their death. These schools or traditions of spirituality have proven their worth simply by surviving the test of time, especially if they have managed to cross historical, geographical and cultural borders.

To preserve such a tradition is not to embalm or fossilise it. A living tradition is never static but fluid, as a river adapts to the contours of the land through which it flows. Indeed, each succeeding generation contributes to, and enriches, the inherited tradition through its own experience, thought, musings and imagination. Authenticity is assured by what is often called 'creative fidelity'. This means that the tradition will always be the same, but it will be creative by evolving over time. Such evolution will normally be gradual, although on occasion a startling reinterpretation may unexpectedly occur. Even in these circumstances, however, the tradition can remain alive and intact, still rooted in and identified with a historical person.

## The Ignatian Tradition

Ignatius Loyola (1491–1556) was one of those specially gifted friends of God who has left a spiritual legacy that endures. He was a charismatic teacher and mentor for those seeking to deepen their relationship with God. For many people during his lifetime and since his death, he has embodied a distinctively holistic way of living the Christian faith. Today his life experiences still speak to ours. His faith-vision engages us as, in some mysterious way, it transcends the centuries. We also know Ignatius as a flawed human being, one who like us experienced moral failures and psychological problems. He always saw himself as in need of God's mercy. The spirituality that we call Ignatian is nothing if not realistic. It is authentically human even as it entices us to taste of the divine. And it is available to everyone: young and old, women and men, ordained and non-ordained. This book explores the spiritual treasure that Ignatius bequeathed to us.

*chapter two*

# Ignatius: Life and Legacy

Born in 1491 into a Basque family of the lower nobility, Ignatius was the youngest of thirteen children. His mother died shortly after his birth and he was fostered for some years in the family of the local blacksmith before returning to the castle of Loyola. At sixteen he left home to become a courtier. For eleven years he acted as a page (*paje*) in the household of Juan Vásquez de Cuéllar in Arévalo. These were followed by four years as a gentleman-at-arms (*gentilhombre*) in the household of the Duke of Nájera who was Viceroy of Navarre.

It was in these surroundings that he developed his enthusiasm for the novels of chivalry, especially the classic *Amadis de Gaul*, and the poetry of courtly love. These novels and poems lauded the values that were identified with chivalry, and they were placed before the young Ignatius as worth living and dying for. Chivalry was, in fact, a curious medieval mix of high and low ideals, of delicate courtesy and a cult of violence. Both the positive and negative aspects affected Ignatius. It is difficult to exaggerate the influence of these fifteen years spent at court during the most formative period of his adolescent and early adult life.

### Conversion and Aftermath

Determined to achieve the same chivalric glory he was reading about in the popular romances of the time, he enthusiastically defended Pamplona against a numerically superior French army in 1521. This daring but foolhardy enterprise did not save the town and led to his being hit by a cannonball that smashed one of his legs and wounded the other. Ignatius was brought back to his family's castle in Loyola where his recovery was long, gruelling and boring. It is quite extraordinary that none of the romances that he craved were kept in the castle during this time; instead, he was unexpectedly drawn to God through the only two books that were available for him to read: a life of Christ, and a collection of lives of the saints.

Through this reading, and by reflecting on the feelings that it aroused in him, Ignatius experienced a deep change within himself – the beginnings of a conversion. A strong desire developed in him to get to know and serve Jesus Christ. This lead to a complete reversal of values, the worldly ones giving way to those of the Gospel. From then on *desires* played a central role in his evolving spirituality. He realised that desires determine the choices we make and how we act.

His new-found fascination with Jesus led to a decision to visit the Holy Land as a poor pilgrim and to pray in those places where Jesus had lived and worked. While preparing for this journey he spent almost a year in a town called Manresa, giving himself to long hours of prayer and practising rigorous fasting and self-denial. He tells us in his *Autobiography* that here God was teaching him as a schoolmaster teaches a child.

He had to learn that the spiritual life does not consist in performing great feats of asceticism – like the mighty deeds performed by heroic knights in the romances of chivalry – but in a discerning love such as he saw Jesus living out in the gospels. As a result, alongside desires, *discerning love* became another foundation stone for what was to come.

Also at Manresa Ignatius sought out people who were willing to speak with him about God. Initially he was looking for help for himself, but he soon discovered that these exchanges were also helpful to others. Consequently, a combination of his own prayer

18 *Towards an Understanding of Ignatian Spirituality*

experiences and his conversations with residents in Manresa became the basis of the *Spiritual Exercises* that he began to write down at this time. He experienced a growing desire 'to help souls' (*aiudar las almas*), and giving the Exercises became his main way of realising this desire. By now he had added a strong apostolic dimension to his spirituality: *to help souls*, or – as we would say today – to help the person or to help others. This became a core value in his life. It is important to note that all this was happening while Ignatius was still a layman.

When Ignatius reached the Holy Land he experienced great joy in fulfilling the normal routines carried out by pilgrims of that era. But he often chose to do so as an individual rather than as part of a group. This led to his disregarding the advice given by the Franciscans who were in charge of the holy places. They were much more conscious than he was of the delicate situation of a Christian minority in territory ruled by Muslims. Breaches of regulations or even conventions could threaten the lives of resident Christians and pilgrims alike. Furthermore, Ignatius wanted to remain permanently in the Holy Land. At a time of great tension in the region this was not acceptable to the Franciscan provincial, who eventually asked Ignatius to leave under threat of excommunication.

## Studies

After returning from the Holy Land Ignatius decided that if he were 'to help souls' he would need to improve his education. He was not without some background, as his training as a courtier had introduced him to the humanities and also given him some practical skills. He had even written some poetry. He was now thirty-three years of age, however, and would have to sit alongside students much younger than he. This was especially so in Barcelona where he began his studies, joining a class of small boys to learn the rudiments of Latin. From there he went on to the Universities of Alcalá and Salamanca, moving eventually to the University of Paris in 1528. Here for eight years he gave himself to philosophy and theology. Although not possessing the mentality of an academic, he performed competently in his studies. He never sought knowledge for its own sake, however; his motivation was always pastoral. His studies were a means enabling him to be more effective in his evangelising of people.

## Companions and Vows

While still in Spain Ignatius had tried to win over some of his fellow-students to his way of thinking and his dreams, but nothing permanent came of his efforts. In Paris, however, he was more successful, winning over a small group of young men, the best known being the Navarrese, Francis Xavier (1506–1552) and the Savoyard, Pierre Favre (1506–1546). On the Feast of the Assumption, 15 August 1534, during a Mass celebrated in a small chapel on Montmartre, the student companions, seven in number, pledged themselves to live in chastity and poverty.

They also promised to go on pilgrimage together to the Holy Land. There was no consensus as to what to do when they arrived there. Some, including Ignatius, would have liked to settle there for the rest of their lives, ministering to the Christians and working for the conversion of the Muslims. If necessary they were willing to accept martyrdom. Others saw themselves returning to Europe once their pilgrimage was over so as to minister there. They all agreed to wait until they were in the Holy Land before making a final decision.

The companions, however, were also politically astute and foresaw that it might prove impossible to get to the Holy Land at all due to Turkish expansionism. They resolved that, if this were to happen, they would travel on to Rome instead and offer their services to the pope. Nevertheless, the Holy Land acted on them like a powerful magnet. Once their studies in Paris were finished, the group – now numbering ten – gathered in Venice, waiting for a pilgrim ship to sail. While there they were all ordained priests, except for Favre who had already been ordained. As they waited,

20  *Towards an Understanding of Ignatian Spirituality*

their hopes of making the pilgrimage were continually frustrated by war between Venice and the Turks. This was showing no signs of abating and was making the Mediterranean a no-go area. After a year-long wait, the companions fell back on their alternative plan and travelled on to Rome.

They travelled in small groups. Ignatius had two companions with him on the journey. As they came within sight of the Eternal City, in a village called La Storta, they stopped off for a rest and to prepare themselves for the final stage of their journey. They went into a small chapel nearby and here Ignatius had one of his mystical visitations. He experienced himself as being 'placed with the Son'.[5] This was in late 1537. The next year they put themselves at the disposal of Pope Paul III.

## Rome and Destiny

How would they have been seen by the authorities in Rome? They were an international group of secular priests, although not belonging to any particular diocese. They were explicitly vowed to a life of poverty and celibacy, and were educated well above the average for clergy of that period. They were energetic and zealous for the spread of the Gospel. The Pope was delighted with their qualities and with their offer to serve.

He soon began to send them in ones and twos to work in different places in Italy. In 1539, realising the need to be clear about their future direction, the companions held a four-month meeting which led to a decision to form a new religious order. They then presented a formal petition to the Pope who approved the foundation of the Society of Jesus – later known as Jesuits – in 1540. Ignatius was elected as the Society's first superior general in the following year.

After so many vicissitudes and travels Ignatius was to spend his last sixteen years in Rome. From there he guided the well-being

5. More will be said about this on 51-54.

of the rapidly expanding order and undertook the writing of its *Constitutions*. He instigated and oversaw apostolic enterprises, first in Italy, then in other European countries, and later throughout the wider world. Much of his time was given to a voluminous correspondence – nearly 7,000 letters of his are extant – that testifies to his dedication and organisational ability. Although no longer a traveller, he continued the most important journey of all, his inner journey that centred on his search for God and the will of God. During this time he was graced with a profound mystical prayer. All of this was accompanied by increasingly bad health. He died on the morning of 31 July 1556. The Society had by then grown to about 1,000 members.

## A Person of Complexity

It must be admitted that an outline of the life of Ignatius, such as I have given, hides as much as it reveals of his character. He was a person of unusual complexity who could reinvent himself time and again. In his own view, of course, this reinvention was God's work in him. He was the clay, God was the potter. We can recall how Jeremiah was instructed by God to visit the potter's house:

> So I went down to the potter's house, and there he was working at his wheel. The vessel he was making of clay was spoiled in the potter's hand, and he reworked it into another vessel, as seemed good to him. Then the word of the Lord came to me. 'Can I not do with you, O house of Israel, just as this potter has done?' says the Lord. Just like the clay in the potter's hand, so are you in my hand, O house of Israel (Jer 18:3-6).

God's constant reworking of Ignatius was hidden and mysterious. It took place deep within him. Its effects can be seen, however, in the radical overturning of his earlier value system at his conversion, as well as in the priorities that he embraced and the decisions that he made in his later life. Focusing exclusively on any one part of his life leads to a distorted, or at best an incomplete, understanding of

## 22 *Towards an Understanding of Ignatian Spirituality*

Ignatius. It is like having a snapshot of a person but without any knowledge of what happened before or after that particular moment in time. Ignatius was always *in fieri*, always in the making, in process, changing, developing.

The complexity of Ignatius's personality has confounded, perturbed and engrossed in equal measure. His friends have tried to resolve the inconsistencies and internal contradictions that they cannot deny, while his enemies have delighted in underscoring, even exaggerating them. This complexity also contributed to the proliferation of legends on both sides of the love/hate divide. Like most legends, these are either totally untrue or they greatly oversimplify Ignatius's portrait. Sometimes – again on either side – they can be a form of propaganda.

Even today scholars continue to struggle to reach an understanding of Ignatius that would satisfy the rigorous criteria of historical research. For example, a recent study by a Swiss Jesuit was subtitled 'Legend and Reality'. It is an updated effort to separate one from the other, the wheat from the chaff.[6] From a very different perspective, an American Jesuit, a practising psychoanalyst, has written two ground-breaking books. The first was a study of Ignatius the man, the second of Ignatian spirituality – both from a psychoanalytical perspective. These works have led to some intriguing hypotheses.[7] The search for 'the real Ignatius' continues.

## Images

One response to complexity is to interpret a person by means of some dominant image. This is meant to get to the heart of who

---

6. Pierre Emonet, SJ, *Ignatius of Loyola: Legend and Reality*, translated by Jerry Ryan, edited by Thomas M. McCoog, SJ. Philadelphia, PA: Saint Joseph's University Press (2016).

7. W. W. Meissner, SJ, MD, *Ignatius of Loyola: The Psychology of a Saint.* New Haven and London: Yale University Press (1992); *To the Greater Glory: A Psychological Study of Ignatian Spirituality.* Milwaukee, WI: Marquette University Press (1999).

this person is, and to convey the identity of the person in an easily recognisable way. Portrait artists have often taken this approach, using a variety of techniques. However, images need not always be pictorial, at least not in a strict sense. They can also be created and transmitted by words, and be as much ideas as pictures. Once an image, of whatever kind, is created and successfully communicated, it can become embedded in our psyche. Then it becomes the filter through which *all* of that person's personality and life are viewed. The dangers of this leading to oversimplification and distortion are obvious. The image ends up being deceptive and manipulative rather than genuinely enlightening.

There have been many images of Ignatius in circulation throughout the centuries. The four most significant are the following.

## Soldier-saint

Since his death in 1556 Ignatius has often been described as a soldier-saint. Some older statues and paintings have even depicted him in battle-dress, sword in hand. This image relates to his family background and his early immersion in the culture of chivalry. Above all it was meant to evoke his military exploits during the futile defence of Pamplona against superior French forces in 1521. The image also recalls his knightly vigil before the statue of the Black Madonna in Montserrat when, en route to Manresa, he left aside his elegant clothes and his armour, committing his loyalty exclusively to Christ.

In turn, these early experiences were often seen as influencing the way in which he structured and organised the Jesuits in his later life. In particular the style of obedience that he required seemed to many to bear the hallmarks of a military model. Jesuits were seen as the 'light cavalry' or the 'shock troops' of the Roman Church, ready to take on the heretics of northern Europe. A soldier-saint and a military-style religious order suited the militant spirit and imagination of the Reformation era. Such a mindset continued during the Tridentine period from the Council of Trent to the Second Vatican Council. The soldier-saint image and its

24  *Towards an Understanding of Ignatian Spirituality*

accompanying ideology won the approval and admiration of Catholics and instilled fear and loathing in Protestants.

Over the last fifty years or so this image has faded, even if it has not totally disappeared. In part, this is because much of what the image conveys has been discredited by historical research. Furthermore, this image does not fit well with our own more irenic and ecumenical attitudes. Respect and dialogue have replaced militancy and the will to overcome. Such dialogue is taking place not only with Christians of other denominations but with other faith traditions as well. In this new context a military image reminds Catholics too uncomfortably of the Crusades, the wars of religion in Europe, and the collusion of the Church in the brutality of the colonial period. In spite of this, the image of Ignatius as a soldier-saint need not be discarded completely.

If we do use it, however, we should remember that a soldier in Ignatius's time and context was not the equivalent of a professional soldier of modern times. It is the chivalrous medieval knight, however idealised, that must be our point of reference. The positive aspects of the ethos of chivalry remained deeply ingrained in Ignatius throughout his life. These included integrity, magnanimity, trustworthiness, service, compassion, bravery, fidelity to a liege lord and dedication to a cause. These values, now transformed by the Gospel, defined, at least in some measure, Ignatius's relationship with Christ and became expressions of his commitment to the reign of God.

## Mystic

This is a favoured image of Ignatius among many of his devotees today. It is grounded in his mystical experiences, especially those in Manresa, La Storta and Rome. There is a growing consensus that this image gets closest to the core of Ignatius, and leads us to appreciate how he found meaning and direction in his life. It also emphasises that his relationship with God was what most made him admirable, and enabled him to teach with such wisdom and authority. From yet another perspective, the image of the mystic resonates with the broader spiritual culture of today, which displays an intensifying curiosity about mysticism.

Once alerted to the weight of this image, we may want to read his *Autobiography* and his *Spiritual Diary* to see what Ignatius reveals of his experiences of God. (We will discuss these texts in subsequent chapters.) Of course, the image of a mystic will never be as concrete or tangible as that of a soldier. We may well have to avoid making it too ethereal or otherworldly. A mystic is not some blithe spirit floating effortlessly above, or even through, the tragicomedy that is life. It is good to have to think deeply about what we actually mean by 'mystic'.

After all, the most frequently quoted statement of the German Jesuit theologian, Karl Rahner, is: 'The Christian of the future will be a mystic or will not exist at all'. It seems that, as Christians, we are all called to be mystics! Perhaps we can be helped by Ignatius.

## Pilgrim

Ignatius's own self-image was much more modest: he was a pilgrim. This is how he referred to himself in the *Autobiography*. It is an image that evokes the inner journey on which God was leading him, but also his many external journeys, especially during his conversion period and his studies. Numerous modern paintings and statues portray Ignatius in shabby pilgrim robes, staff in hand, ever in motion, on his quest for God.

There is something in this image that appeals strongly to people today. In a world full of animosity, violence and uncertainty, we humans are fragile creatures, often unsure of our own identity or purpose. We see ourselves as incomplete, always in process of becoming but never fulfilled. We travel but never arrive. Yet we have no choice but to keep moving even if we seem to be going around in circles or climbing a descending escalator. In religious terms we are experiencing our own poverty. Some may live in denial and flaunt their imagined wealth and power. But many, in

26  *Towards an Understanding of Ignatian Spirituality*

one way or another, come to recognise that they are needy pilgrims on this earth and, like Ignatius, learn to trust in God alone.

The anthropologists, Victor and Edith Turner, help us to bring together in an intriguing way the images of the mystic and pilgrim. They write from their professional expertise:

> Pilgrimage may be thought of as extroverted mysticism, just as mysticism is introverted pilgrimage. The pilgrim physically traverses a mystical way; the mystic sets forth on an interior spiritual pilgrimage. For the former, concreteness and historicity dominate; for the latter, a phased interior process leads to a goal beyond conceptualisation.[8]

It is not difficult to see how these insights can be applied to Ignatius whom we have come to know as both mystic and as a pilgrim.

## Management Guru

This is probably the least influential, even least well-known, of the four images. It stems from a high regard for the way that Ignatius led the newly founded but fast-growing Society of Jesus during the last sixteen years of his life. Simultaneously, as we have seen, he was composing the *Constitutions* of the order.

Professionals in the field of management and business studies have regarded the *Constitutions* as a masterpiece for delivering effective management in an organisation. Whether one regards Ignatius as Spirit-filled or Machiavellian in their composition, as well as in his own leadership, will depend in large part on one's prior suppositions. Perhaps he was both!

In truth Ignatius, because of his multi-layered personality, needs all these images – and perhaps more – to be in operation and to

---

8. Victor Turner and Edith Turner, *Image and Pilgrimage in Christian Culture: Anthropological Perspectives.* Oxford: Basil Blackwell (1978), 33-34.

complement each other. He *was* a soldier-saint, a mystic, a pilgrim and a management guru. Each image is a valid though incomplete description of his character and what he achieved. And each will have its role to play as we discuss more deeply the dynamic of his life and spirituality.

## Spiritual Exercises

There will be many references, implicit and explicit, to the Spiritual Exercises in coming chapters. These Exercises are the chief means through which Ignatius continues to share his own journey, and the wisdom that he learned from it, with succeeding generations. A short introduction will be in order here.

Many people, hearing about this famous book, have taken it up and tried to read through it from beginning to end. They have been puzzled by its layout, mystified by its lack of sophistication and ultimately sorely disappointed. If they are willing to consult someone familiar with the Ignatian tradition, however, the first lesson they will learn is that this book is not to be compared with works such as *The Way of Perfection* of St Teresa of Avila or *An Introduction to the Devout Life* by St Francis de Sales. The Exercises are to be *made* rather than read. Ignatius himself offers the best explanation:

> By the term Spiritual Exercises we mean every method of examination of conscience, meditation, contemplation, vocal or mental prayer, and other spiritual activities, such as will be mentioned later. For, just as taking a walk, travelling on foot, and running are physical exercises, so is the name of spiritual exercises given to any means of preparing and disposing our soul to rid itself of all its disordered affections and then, after their removal, of seeking and finding God's will in the ordering of our life for the salvation of our soul [SE 1].

The book outlines these exercises and offers advice as to how best to present them to another person. It is, therefore, a handbook

28  *Towards an Understanding of Ignatian Spirituality*

for the one who accompanies or guides or directs another – the present-day terminology is fluid. Indeed, Ignatius did not even want the person making the Exercises to have a copy of the book!

One who chooses to make the Exercises is often said to be on retreat. This person is then called a retreatant, although the more correct term is exercitant, meaning one who is engaged in exercising.

Besides, the word 'retreat' is ambiguous, because making the Exercises is a retreat of a unique kind. There are no talks or exhortations and, apart from the daily Eucharist, no devotional practices in common with a group. Instead the focus is on allowing *you*, the unique individual, the space to reflect, to pray, to listen to what God may be saying in *your* life. The exercitant remains in silence throughout except for a daily meeting with a director. The full Spiritual Exercises last for thirty days, more or less. They are usually made in a quiet place such as a retreat house, often in an attractive location.

The Exercises can also be made in daily life, however. This means that a person continues living and working as normal, but puts time aside each day for prayer. In this mode, the full Exercises may last for up to a year. Regular – usually weekly – meetings with a spiritual director offer the necessary support, particularly with help in discernment.

Shorter adaptations of the Exercises are also possible, such as the six- or eight-day retreat that religious, and an increasing number of lay people, make on a more-or-less annual basis. Shorter retreats of three or four days, or over a weekend, may be said to provide a taster of what the longer Exercises offer.

Many other creative adaptations have been developed in recent years. Some of these, especially when offered to younger people, include a communal dimension.

## Structure

The dynamic of the Spiritual Exercises moves through four stages which are referred to in the text as 'weeks'. This terminology can be misleading, since the periods are of unequal length and do not correspond with calendar weeks. In outline their subject matter is as follows.

### Week 1

The focus is on human sinfulness and God's mercy. The subject is approached in a variety of ways, from meditating on the sin of the angels and that of Adam and Eve, to the exercitant's own sin-history. The overarching grace being sought is to experience oneself as a forgiven sinner, embraced by a merciful God, as in Rembrandt's painting of the Prodigal Son.

### Week 2

This begins with the Incarnation, and moves on to contemplations on the Infancy Narratives and the public life of Jesus. The grace sought will be 'an interior knowledge of Our Lord, who became human for me, that I may love him more intensely and follow him more closely' [104]. The exercitant prays to grow into a deeply personal relationship with Jesus, the Word made flesh.

### Week 3

This involves being with Jesus as he moves through his Passion, staying with him to the end. The exercitant prays for 'sorrow with Christ in sorrow; a broken spirit with Christ so broken; tears; and interior suffering because of the great suffering which Christ endured for me' [203]. This may be the time when the exercitant is most vulnerable, helpless and stretched.

### Week 4

This is given over to being with Christ in his risen glory. The grace sought will be 'to be glad and to rejoice intensely because of the great glory and joy of Christ our Lord' [221]. Taken together, Weeks 3 and 4 draw us into the fullness of the Paschal Mystery, the dying and rising of Jesus, which becomes our own dying and rising.

30    *Towards an Understanding of Ignatian Spirituality*

The four 'Weeks' are punctuated by other exercises composed by Ignatius himself. Best known are the Call of the King (or the Kingdom), the Two Standards and the Contemplation to Attain Love. These are not directly scripture-based although, with some knowledge and imagination, they can be presented in scriptural terms.

They help to focus the dynamic of the Exercises at certain key moments.

## The Election

The last constitutive part of the Exercises that I will mention here is what Ignatius calls the election. This is the term that he uses for the process of decision-making, which usually takes place within Week 2. In this context, it is worth noting that, as well as his description of the Exercises already given, Ignatius added another:

> Spiritual Exercises to overcome oneself and to order one's life without reaching a decision through some disordered affection [SE 21].

The election is the nucleus of the dynamic that is at work in the Spiritual Exercises. Many commentators regard the election as their main purpose. Even those exercitants who are not aware of having any major decision to make can profit greatly from moving through the election process. It enables them to continue growing in self-knowledge, and above all in inner freedom. This empowers them to take a new look at their lives and to reassess their priorities. They become more committed to respond to whatever God is doing in their lives.

The Spiritual Exercises are the greatest legacy left by Ignatius to the Church. This brief introduction has provided an opportunity to explain certain technical terms that appear in the text and are in common use in Ignatian spirituality. It may also have answered some of the questions that arise for those unfamiliar with the

Exercises. Later references to this text should be clearer as a result and allow the reader to situate them within the structure we have outlined. But now let us move on to another starting point and begin a new exploration.

*chapter three*

# *Acta Patris Ignatii:*
# The Autobiography

Anyone who shows an interest in learning about Ignatian spirituality is likely to be encouraged to read his *Autobiography*. This short book of reminiscences covers the middle years of Ignatius's life, from his wounding at Pamplona in 1521 to the persecution of the early companions in Rome in 1538. This was the period during which his spirituality was taking on a recognisable shape. The narrative is quite easy to read, and in many ways it is also dramatic. Ignatius's life, as we learn from the *Autobiography*, was by no means trouble-free. It was laced with challenges from psychic forces within himself, as well as from opponents and other external obstacles. We see how he moved through the three traditional stages of the spiritual life: purgative (purification from sin and other unfreedoms); illuminative (enlightenment by God's Spirit); and unitive (union with God, especially in his mystical experiences).

## Potential of Story

In recent times we have become more aware of the potential of story to be a carrier of revelation. In the Christian tradition we have the story-telling that makes up so much of the Old Testament, the Gospels and the Acts of the Apostles, and we also have those later stories of the saints that have played an important role in popular piety. Contemporary enquirers find in story a lively and experiential way of learning about the mysterious interaction of God with his people. Stories can attract, instruct and influence those who hear them.

They do this, not by communicating truth in an abstract way, or by being didactic, but simply by inviting readers to enter imaginatively into another person's experience. This then allows readers to get in touch with their own personal story, sometimes bringing to the surface not just memories but even aspects of the subconscious. Indeed, readers often feel that they are learning as much about their own lives as about the life of the story's protagonist. Such is the power of story. The story-telling that most interests us here can be in the form of either biography or autobiography. These genres do not always exist in a pure form, however: we have only to think of authorised and unauthorised biographies, for example, and autobiographies that are written by a ghost-writer. It may be more realistic to talk of writings that contain biographical or autobiographical elements. This broadens the categories and allows us to include diaries, journals, letters, jottings and even recorded conversations.

Leaving aside such distinctions, however, we would normally place works such as James Boswell's *The Life of Samuel Johnson* (1791) under the heading of biography; and under autobiography we would list Anne Frank's *The Diary of a Young Girl* (1947) and Nelson Mandela's *Long Walk to Freedom* (1995). To simplify even more, a biography will tell the story of a person other than the author, while an autobiography will tell the author's own story. A biography will be written in the third person, an autobiography in the first.

## Puzzling Aspects

Having heard the work we are discussing called the *Autobiography* of Ignatius, most readers take this description at face value. They presume that its genre is familiar to them. Yet even in a first perusing of the text they are more than likely to notice aspects of the

34  *Towards an Understanding of Ignatian Spirituality*

work that are puzzling. If this is an autobiography, why is the story told in the third person? Did Ignatius not write the text himself? Did he have a ghost writer? Furthermore, why did he begin his life story with the siege of Pamplona, when he was thirty years of age, rather than with his birth? Has part of the text been lost? Why did he end the narrative in 1538, given he lived quite a bit beyond that? Have we any idea why Ignatius chose to share these reminiscences? Had he some hidden agenda? The background to the *Autobiography* seems more complicated than its content! We will examine some of these questions, not as an academic exercise, but to deepen our understanding of what Ignatius intended to communicate.

The original title of this work was simply *Acta Patris Ignatii* (Acts of Father Ignatius) and from now on that is the title I will use in referring to this text. The term *Acta* may seem vague and even enigmatic to us. Sixteenth-century readers would immediately recognise the implied comparison with the Acts of the Apostles. Those *Acta*, written by the evangelist Luke, describe the life of the early Christian communities in Jerusalem and elsewhere. Besides, they record the memorable conversion and missionary journeys of St Paul. More accurately, however, Luke is portraying how the Holy Spirit guided and energised the early Christians, both Jewish and Gentile, as well as driving Paul to proclaim the gospel in season and out of season. Might this throw light on what the *Acta Patris Ignatii* was aiming to do in the case of Ignatius? Many interpreters think so. Paul and Ignatius have much in common.

## Authorship

A more difficult question concerns the authorship of the text. The use of the third person throughout may lead us to suspect that this is a biography rather than an autobiography. Again the word *Acta* offers no clarification. To complicate matters further, the text has a fuller title that adds the words 'written by Father Luís Gonçalvez da Câmara'. A definite attribution, certainly, but still highly ambiguous. Does it mean that the text was composed by da Câmara? Or was da Câmara a redactor? Or simply a scribe? What was the working relationship between Ignatius and da Câmara? Fortunately, help is at hand. The original text of the *Acta* is accompanied by two prefaces or prologues that help us to understand its genesis and purpose: how it was envisaged; who played a role in instigating the project; the manner in which the *Acta* was composed; difficulties along the way; and the motivation of Ignatius in allowing his life-story to be made public, specifically among Jesuits. The prefaces answer most of the questions that we have raised, and in so doing orient our reading of the text.

## Nadal's Preface

The figure of Jerome Nadal (1507-1580) looms large in any consideration of the *Acta*. This close confidant of Ignatius had been entrusted with the task of promulgating the *Constitutions* in the Jesuit communities around Europe. On these journeys he was inevitably expected to speak also about Ignatius himself. Most Jesuits had never met the founder – or co-founder – of their order and were naturally keen to know what sort of person he was. But what was Nadal to say? Ignatius had never given a full account of his life to anyone since he had become superior general in 1541. The first companions knew more than most, but they were now a small minority in a fast growing and widely scattered Society. In any case Nadal was not one of them, having only entered the Society in 1545. He needed to get Ignatius to open up and reveal himself in a way that he had never done before. Nadal was also aware that time was not on his side. Ignatius was in bad health, had nearly died in 1550, and could pass away at any time. There was an urgency about the matter.

One day in August 1551 Ignatius was talking with Nadal and, quite out of the blue, said, 'Just now I was higher than heaven'. Nadal presumed that Ignatius was referring to an ecstasy or rapture that he had just experienced, and out of an understandable curiosity, he asked, 'Father, what do you mean?' But at once Ignatius

36  *Towards an Understanding of Ignatian Spirituality*

changed the conversation, perhaps regretting that he had mentioned the occurrence at all. Nadal goes on:

> Thinking that this was the suitable moment, I begged the Father to be kind enough to tell us how the Lord had guided him from the beginning of his conversion, so that his explanation could serve us as a testament and paternal instruction. Thus, I said to him: 'Since God has granted you the three graces you desired before your death, we fear, Father, that you will soon be called to heaven' [AIP 2].

The graces that Nadal was referring to were the Pope's confirmation of the Society of Jesus (1540 and 1550); the parallel confirmation of the Spiritual Exercises (1548); and Ignatius's near-completion of the *Constitutions* (in fact finalised in the following year, 1552). These desires of Ignatius had all come to pass. It is as though Nadal is hinting to Ignatius that he now has nothing of major importance left to live for. As a result he will probably die soon and be brought to heaven. So he had better tell his story *now*!

Ignatius initially excused himself on the grounds of being too busy. He then compromised somewhat by instructing Nadal, Juan de Polanco (Ignatius's highly efficient secretary and personal assistant), and Ponce Cogardon (the house treasurer) to offer three Masses and to pray to know what he, Ignatius, should do about this matter. When they had fulfilled these instructions, the three priests reported back to Ignatius that, in their judgement, he *should* tell the story of God's dealings with him. Ignatius then promised to comply.

Almost two years later, early in 1553, when Nadal returned to Rome after a visit to Sicily, he asked Ignatius if he had done anything about this undertaking. Ignatius replied, 'Nothing'. The following year, this time after returning from Spain, Nadal again confronted Ignatius and got a similar reply. He was becoming more and more exasperated with the passing of time. Now, however, learning from his earlier failures, he took a different approach.

*Acta Patris Ignatii: The Autobiography*  37

I do not know what impelled me, but I insisted with the Father, 'It is now going on four years that not only have I asked you, but also other fathers, for you to explain to us, Father, how the Lord had formed you from the beginning of your conversion, for we are confident that knowing this would be most beneficial to us and to the Society. But since I see that you will not grant it to us, I dare to make this statement: If you grant the request we so earnestly desire, we will put it to our best use, and if you do not grant it, our spirits will not be thereby dejected, but we will have the same confidence in the Lord as if you had written everything down' [AIP 3].

This expression of 'indifference' – inner freedom, spiritual freedom[9] – on Nadal's part may well have been genuine on a conscious level, but it was also a cleverly manipulative ploy. Having failed so often with a frontal assault, Nadal's new approach had the effect of disarming Ignatius and of softening his resistance. Nadal's real – or feigned? – indifference created for Ignatius a psychological space out of which he could respond freely, without feeling coerced. That very day, or soon afterwards, Ignatius began to tell his story.[10]

## Da Câmara's Preface

Nadal's phrase, 'as if you had written everything down', indicates that he expected Ignatius to *write* his life-story. Ignatius, however, chose to *dictate* it. It is not clear why he made this decision, but we might speculate that dictation seemed less time consuming than writing. It may also have been a subconscious form of protest, part

---

9. See *Spiritual Exercises*, 23.

10. There is a confusion of dates here that is impossible to disentangle. See da Câmara's preface. Nadal wrote his preface sometime between 1561 and 1576, many years after the death of Ignatius. It is not surprising that his memory may have been faulty. Da Câmara had written his preface before the death of Ignatius in 1556.

# 38 *Towards an Understanding of Ignatian Spirituality*

of his ongoing resistance to the whole idea of self-revelation. This resistance manifested itself also in a series of procrastinations over the following months, which might suggest a passive-aggressive reaction.

The man Ignatius selected as the recipient of his oral communication was Luís Gonçalves da Câmara (1520-1575), a Portuguese Jesuit who had come to Rome only two months earlier. He had been appointed administrator in the house where Ignatius lived.[11] Da Câmara's preface begins with a conversation he had with Ignatius on 4 August 1553. It took place in a garden attached to the house. He was opening his soul to Ignatius and, among other matters, he spoke of his temptations to vainglory. The Father, as da Câmara always calls Ignatius, offered him advice and consolation 'and as a result I could not hold back my tears'. He continues,

> The Father then told me how for two years he had struggled against this vice and with such effort that, when he was about to set sail from Barcelona for Jerusalem, he dared not tell anyone that he was going to Jerusalem, and he did the same in other circumstances. He added, with regard to this matter, that great peace of soul was his ever afterwards [AIP 1].

The struggle with vainglory was a common thread binding the two men. It seems to have influenced Ignatius in his choice of da Câmara as his trusted listener. It is surely not without significance that, in the very first sentence of the *Acta*, the pilgrim describes himself as then – before the Pamplona escapade – 'having a vain

---

11. Later he was to publish a diary that he kept from January to August 1555 in which he recorded in detail the actions, words and attitudes of Ignatius as he observed them in that Roman house. He idealised Ignatius, finding goodness and wisdom even in some of Ignatius's arbitrary ways of governing. See *Remembering Iñigo: Glimpses of the Life of Saint Ignatius of Loyola. The 'Memoriale' of Luis Gonçalves da Câmara*, translated with introduction, notes and indices by Alexander Eaglestone and Joseph A. Munitiz, SJ. Leominster: Gracewing Publishing/ Saint Louis: Institute of Jesuit Sources (2005).

and overpowering desire to gain renown'. This ongoing battle of Ignatius with vainglory, which lasted much longer than the two years to which he had confessed, is also the most plausible explanation for his idiosyncratic decision to dictate his story in the third person. He did not want to build the narrative around the 'I'. The *Acta* was not to be an exercise in self-promotion. God was to be the story's central character, not Ignatius.

Da Câmara resumes:

> An hour or two later we were at dinner, and while Master Polanco and I were eating with him, our Father said that many times Master Nadal and others of the Society had made a special request of him, but he had never come to any decision about it. Now, after having spoken with me, and having gone to his room, he felt a powerful inclination and desire to fulfil that request, and – speaking in such a way that it was clear that God had inspired him to see what his duty was – he was now determined to do it, that is, narrate all that had happened in his soul up to the present time, and he likewise decided that I was to be the one to whom he would reveal these matters [AIP 1].

In spite of that 'powerful inclination and desire', Ignatius did not begin immediately, but used his ill health or urgent business as excuses to justify the further delay. Finally, in early September he summoned da Câmara to join him and started to dictate. Later that same month he sent for him three or four times and brought the narrative up to his first days in Manresa. At this point there is another gap, lasting up to March 1555, eighteen months later. Even then, a projected new start was interrupted by the death of Pope Julius III, followed shortly by the death of his successor Pope Marcellus II, and the election of Cardinal Carafa as Pope Paul IV. Then, besides additional urgent business, Ignatius used the heat of that summer as a pretext for yet another deferral. It was not until late September that year that the narrative was resumed, and then only because da Câmara was about to leave for Spain. The final interview took place on the eve of his departure.

40  *Towards an Understanding of Ignatian Spirituality*

In summary, there were three periods of dictation: September 1553, March 1555, and September-October 1555. The initial request, at least the earliest we know of, was made by Nadal in 1551. So we are dealing with a time-span of four years! Almost predictably, nine months after he ended his narration, Ignatius died.

## Composition

How did the text come to be as we have it? Firstly, as we have seen, Ignatius would summon da Câmara to meet him. He would then dictate the part of his story that he had chosen for that day, while pacing up and down the room. Da Câmara would listen, not asking any questions, not seeking any clarification and not taking any notes. He simply listened until Ignatius dismissed him. Da Câmara then went away and made brief summary notes of what he had heard. Sometime later (we do not know how much later) he wrote up these notes more fully. Then he, in turn, dictated what he had written to a scribe who then recorded it. In Rome, da Câmara used a number of different scribes who could work in Spanish, which was the language used by Ignatius.

After the final session, however, he only had time to make his initial summary notes in Spanish before having to set out from Rome. He had to wait till he arrived in Genoa before writing up his fuller version. There, since he could not find a scribe who was familiar with Spanish, he was forced to write this fuller version in Italian and dictate it in that language.

We can see that there were many steps between Ignatius's speaking and the final text of the *Acta*. Given this sequence of stages, the time span involved, and the human factors that inevitably came into play throughout the entire process, it is not plausible to claim that the text enshrines the exact words of Ignatius. Yet that is what most commentators used to believe, acting on the flawed assumption that the *Acta* is an autobiography. They also appealed to what da Câmara wrote in his preface, although not adverting sufficiently to the nuances in his claims:

I have tried not to write a single word other than those that I heard from the Father, and with regard to those where I fear I have failed it is because, not wanting to depart from the Father's words, I have not been able to properly explain the force of some of them [AIP 3].

Da Câmara enjoyed a reputation of having an excellent memory, and there is no reason to doubt this. Indeed it would have been strange if Ignatius had chosen someone with a contrary reputation. What did having an excellent memory mean in the context of his times? During the Renaissance, to say that someone had an excellent memory was primarily a tribute to that person's *integrity*. Here is someone who would not deviate from the substance of what they had heard. Beyond that, here is someone with the skill to distil that substance and to relay the meaning that the speaker intended. It does *not* imply an ability to remember word for word what has been said. This is another reason why the claim that the *Acta* gives us Ignatius in his own words cannot be justified. It does, however, give us the *substance* of what he said, but, to an unknown extent, in the words of da Câmara. Of course, there may well be many expressions, or even whole sentences, in the *Acta* exactly as spoken by Ignatius. Even so, it will be impossible to distinguish these from da Câmara's paraphrases.[12]

## Purpose of the Acta

One of the questions that we have raised, and to some extent answered, concerns the purpose behind the *Acta*. Understanding this will teach us how best to set about using the work as a spiritual resource. We now return to this issue in more depth, again drawing on the two prefaces.

---

12. For a discussion of this and related matters, on which I have drawn here, see Marjorie O'Rourke Boyle, *Loyola's Acts: The Rhetoric of the Self*. Berkeley/Los Angeles/London: University of California Press (1997), 1-21.

42  *Towards an Understanding of Ignatian Spirituality*

Let us first examine this statement of Nadal:

> Since I knew that the holy father-founders of monastic communities had been accustomed to leave their sons some admonition, as a testament, to help them grow in virtue, I waited for the opportune moment to ask the same of Father Ignatius [AIP 2].

The key word here is 'testament'. Nadal was hoping for a document similar to the *Testament* of St Francis of Assisi, which was treasured within the Franciscan family. Within the text itself, Francis had described it as 'a remembrance, an admonition, an exhortation, and my testament'. This was the best-known of many such testaments left to their followers by founders of religious orders. Nadal wanted Ignatius to leave behind him words that would provide enlightenment, guidance and encouragement for Jesuits who would feel bereft at his death. Furthermore, this was to be a way for Ignatius to continue living on among his followers, even into future generations. Further on in the prologue – in a passage already quoted – Nadal had written:

> I begged the Father to be kind enough to tell us how the Lord had guided him from the beginning of his conversion, so that his explanation could serve us as a testament and paternal instruction [AIP 2].

We note here the repetition of the key word 'testament'. But now Nadal is specifying that the core of this testament is to be a narrative of how God guided Ignatius from the beginning of his conversion. Note where the stress lies. It is to be the story of *God's* initiative and *God's* involvement in his life. He is not looking for, as we would understand it, an autobiography. Throughout the rest of his life Nadal kept returning to his basic conviction, stressing its crucial importance for the well-being of the Society of Jesus. He was later to write, 'The Society develops in the same way as the life of our Father unfolded'. In other words, God will lead the Society according to the same pattern that he wove into the life of Ignatius. Hence the urgent need to have Ignatius's account of how God led him. This would provide a prototype for the future. Without it, Jesuits would be without a compass as they navigated the ocean of life. Consider also a statement attributed to Nadal by da Câmara in his own preface:

> When Father Nadal arrived he was very happy to see that the project was begun and told me to urge the Father to continue, telling me many times that the Father could do nothing better for the Society than this, and that this was truly to give the Society its foundations (*y que esto era fundar verdaderamente la Compañia*) [AIP 4].

This assertion of Nadal's is in line with the others quoted earlier, yet it is even more radical. He argues that, without having Ignatius's own version of his story, the Society would be without a foundation. He may even be claiming that for Ignatius to tell the story of God's dealings with him was *to found or establish* the Society; the Spanish is more blunt than its English translation. Nadal's rhetoric may have led him into some exaggeration here. The Society had already been founded, and papal approval granted in 1540 and again in 1550, but Nadal is articulating a pervasive insight, the truth of which has become more evident over time.

Still more intriguing is that Ignatius himself held views that were similar to Nadal's. Of course, they were expressed more simply and without any rhetorical flourish. According to Diego Laynez (1512-1565), one of the first companions and the one who succeeded Ignatius as superior general:

> Father Ignatius used to say that when God chooses someone to be the founder of a religious order, he leads him in such a way as he wishes those who follow him to walk also.

This statement sums up the purpose of the *Acta* in a single sentence, even if it needs some teasing out. But it also makes Ignatius's resistance to telling his story all the more puzzling.

## Movement

We conclude these considerations by signposting one of the themes which, when identified, facilitates a reading of the *Acta*. This is the theme of *movement*. From his conversion onwards movement played a central role in the spirituality of Ignatius. While convalescing from his wounds at Loyola, he noticed how different spirits moved him, or in more colloquial terms, how his moods changed. Through reflecting on this experience he learned the rudiments of discernment. Later, during the eleven months that he stayed in Manresa, Ignatius was exposed to the increasingly subtle movements of the spirits and was taught by God how to decipher them. The descriptions of consolation and desolation that he wrote into the *Spiritual Exercises* [316, 317] can, according to many commentators, be best understood in terms of inner movements: consolation, drawing us towards God, and desolation, drawing us away from God.

There was also external, physical movement involved, arising from his decision to embrace the life of a pilgrim. Ignatius began to move from town to town, from country to country, in a constant search for the will of God and for opportunities to carry it out. In the pages of the *Acta* he travels along many roads – most often on foot – as well as sailing the seas. Some journeys were apparently futile because they did not lead to what he was seeking. Occasionally his progress was blocked by military or civilian authorities. But Ignatius was persistent, never giving up, and never making himself at home in any halfway house. There was always further movement, because there was always further searching to carry out. A recurring question he asks in the *Acta* is '*Quid agendum?*' What is to be done now? What next? The movement must continue, for the greater glory of God.

As Ignatius increased in spiritual sensitivity he recognised that, for all his own energy and determination, he was not the main mover in the drama of his life. There was another Mover at work, who was more powerful and dynamic and farseeing than himself.

The Trinitarian God was continually moving to meet Ignatius, encouraging him to synchronise his movement with God's. It was as if God were inviting Ignatius to take part with him in a dance through life. Good dancers dance for each other and have a fluidity of movement that is always sensitive to that of their partner. There is a premium on mutuality: a mutuality of attention, of intention and of rhythm. This image of the dance allows for the divine initiative, human cooperation, and the gradual at-onement of Ignatius with God. All of this will become clearer as we examine the mysticism of Ignatius in the next chapter.

*chapter four*

# Mystical Gifts

Fresh from his initial conversion at Loyola, Ignatius spent eleven months in Manresa (1522-23). He was on his way to the Holy Land as a pilgrim and initially intended to spend no more than a couple of days in the town, but something held him there, and his stay turned out to be transformative in his life. From his *Acta* we can distinguish three different phases of contrasting experiences:

> April to May were days of light, during which he was gifted with peace and joy. This was a kind of honeymoon period, often associated with the immediate aftermath of a conversion. In his innocence he thought that it would last forever!
>
> May to the end of July were days of darkness, during which he struggled with doubts and other kinds of desolation, culminating in a devastating battle with scruples. These were so severe that he even considered suicide. He was certainly being brought down to earth.
>
> August to mid-February were days of glory, during which God gifted him with a series of mystical experiences. These were so profound that he would often refer back to them in later life, especially at times of serious decision-making.

Mysticism, which is nearly impossible to define, has something to do with the experience of God. But can God be experienced? Some readers may have been brought up to answer 'no' to this question. God is pure spirit, invisible, intangible, and so forth. God

*Mystical Gifts*   47

is Wholly Other, like nothing we have experienced or can experience on the human level. We come to know him only by faith, which is a kind of darkness, a kind of 'unknowing'. And yet . . . there have always been Christians who claim to have had an experience of God, to have come to know him personally, even to have an intimate relationship with him. Such men and women can even tell us something of what God is like, or at least what he is like for them. They may only be able to convey this in stumbling, halting words, or in obscure metaphors or symbols, or through the medium of art. But we sense that these people are pointing to a God they know, who is real for them, whom they have experienced in their lives. This is not necessarily the vocation of the few, of an elite. The call to be a mystic, at least in a broad sense, is as inclusive as the universal call to holiness.

## Peak Experiences

There are, of course, different levels on which people experience God, as well as a range of intensities. Using Abraham Maslow's term, some may have 'peak experiences' of God from time to time. Ignatius was gifted with many such mystical encounters that were beyond the ordinary. The *Acta* records that during his time in Manresa he had a series of five such experiences. He introduces them by saying:

> During this period God was dealing with him in the same way a schoolteacher deals with a child while instructing him. This was because either he was thick and dull of brain, or because of the firm will that God himself had implanted in him to serve him – but he clearly recognised and has always recognised that it was in this way that God dealt with him. Furthermore, if he were to doubt this, he would think he was offending the Divine Majesty [AIP 27].

So it is with great assurance and conviction that he gives an account of the revelations that he had received those many years

## 48 Towards an Understanding of Ignatian Spirituality

earlier. He describes them as an understanding of the Trinity; of how God created the world; and of how Christ is present in the Eucharist. These were followed by a vision of the humanity of Christ, and a vision of Our Lady. It is not necessary to see them as occurring in this precise order, though there may be a certain prioritising in the list on the basis of their effect on him – then and later. Especially significant is his giving first place to his experience of the Trinity.

> One day, as he was saying the Hours of Our Lady on the monastery's steps, his understanding was raised on high, so as to see the Most Holy Trinity under the aspect of three keys on a musical instrument, and as a result he shed many tears and sobbed so strongly that he could not control himself . . . This experience remained with him for the rest of his life so that whenever he prayed to the Most Holy Trinity he felt great devotion [AIP 28].

Having described the five mystical gifts, Ignatius ends by stating:

> These things he saw at that time fortified him and gave such great support to his faith that many times he thought to himself: if there were no scriptures to teach us these matters of faith, he would still resolve to die for them on the basis of what he had seen [AIP 29].

We need not be discouraged when we read of the extraordinary experiences of mystics such as Ignatius. God treats every person, just as he treated him, 'in the same way a schoolteacher deals with a child'. Like any good teacher God adapts his instruction to our unique personality, our capacity and our needs. Besides, not all experiences of God need be 'peak experiences'. For large parts of his own life Ignatius was undoubtedly 'off-peak'. Maybe we will be that way all of the time! Nevertheless, as we move through life, attentive to God in prayer, and serving him through our relationships and daily activities, God is gradually revealing to us also something of what Ignatius learned at Manresa.

Quietly, almost secretly, God discloses within us the mystery of the Trinity (God is a community), of creation (God made all things good), of the Eucharist (God shares his life with us), of Christ's humanity (Jesus is like us in all things except sin), and of Our Lady (given to us on Calvary as our mother). This is not some abstract theological thinking but a self-revelation by God that invites us into a deeper relationship with him. Listening, paying attention, accepting this invitation, responding with the gift of ourselves – this is to experience God, to become a mystic in everyday life.

## Cardoner

The five experiences of Ignatius that we have been considering were surpassed in depth and impact by another, known as the 'great enlightenment'. It took place on the banks of the river Cardoner that flows through Manresa and is best described in the words of the *Acta*:

> He was once on his way, out of devotion, to a church a little more than a mile from Manresa, which I think was called Saint Paul. The road followed the path of the river and he was taken up with his devotions; he sat down for a while facing the river flowing far below him As he sat there the eyes of his understanding were opened and, though he saw no vision, he understood and perceived many things, numerous spiritual things as well as matters touching on faith and learning, and this was with an elucidation so bright that all these things seemed new to him. He cannot expound in detail what he then understood, for they were many things, but he can state that he received such a lucidity in understanding that during the course of his entire life – now having passed his sixty-second year – if he were to gather all the helps he received from God and everything he knew, and add them together, he does not think they would add up to all that he received on that one occasion [AIP 30].

While the Cardoner experience is the greatest enlightenment received by Ignatius from God, the content of this enlightenment is difficult to determine. He speaks of being given to understand 'numerous spiritual things as well as matters touching on faith and learning'. But what were they? He does not specify. Probably – though by no means certainly – he was not being taught *new* truths but was seeing familiar ones in a more penetrating light, so that they '*seemed* new to him'. And since he recalls the Cardoner experience immediately after his description of the five earlier visions, it is at least conceivable that he received inter alia a still deeper understanding of the Trinity, Creation, Eucharist, the humanity of Christ and Our Lady. But this is speculation.

However, there is one surprising aspect to the Cardoner experience that merits special attention. It concerns the mention of 'matters touching on faith and learning'. Rare, if not unique, is the inclusion of learning in the subject-matter of a mystical experience. The Spanish word *letras* that Ignatius uses makes it clear that he is referring to secular learning. Its inclusion indicates, or at least suggests, that he was enabled to grasp the interrelatedness or interconnectedness of all truth, bringing together matters of the spirit, of faith and of secular learning. Nadal wrote that at the Cardoner Ignatius saw 'the guiding principles and causes of all things'. He was given to understand how all things – secular as well as sacred, earthly as well as heavenly, natural as well as supernatural – have their starting point and end point in the one creator God.

This interpretation of the Cardoner experience helps us to understand, even if obscurely, how it bore fruit in Ignatius as the gift of discernment. We are told by his contemporaries that Cardoner became for him the touchstone in all his future decision-making. It was a beacon that shone its light on all the complexities that he faced, especially in times of crisis. There will be more on discernment in the next chapter.

## Christian Humanism

Grasping the interrelatedness of truth also allowed Ignatius to elaborate a spirituality that may broadly be termed humanistic.

*Mystical Gifts*   51

The words 'humanism' and 'humanistic', while frequently applied to Ignatian spirituality today, are somewhat problematical. Ignatius was certainly not a humanist in the modern sense, where the term has been become almost synonymous with atheistic secular humanism. But neither was he a humanist in *any* way that would place the human person rather than God at the centre of the universe. Ignatius's world-view was intuitively theocentric, or God-centred, and this was reinforced at the Cardoner.

For Ignatius, God is the ultimate reference-point for all of reality. He is 'God Ever Greater', which is the title I have chosen for this book. So I use the word humanist of Ignatius with a certain caution. It is simply meant to indicate his appreciation, even reverence, for the whole of creation – he would be an enthusiastic environmentalist today! – and his valuing of the human person with all the associated gifts, talents and creativity. It also suggests his conviction that we must cultivate the human as well as worship the divine. It is not difficult to see how all this would later lead Ignatius and his order into the apostolate of education. Scholarship, research and the teaching of secular subjects were to be embraced as a tribute to God who made such an astonishing world, and with the conviction that the truth we seek in any particular area will always be a mirror of the one truth.

While Ignatius was certainly drawn into the mystery of the divine, his Cardoner experience simultaneously plunged him more deeply into the mystery of the human. From then on his thinking always sought to bring together these two polarities – the divine and the human – all to the greater glory of God.

## La Storta

We now move from the year 1522 in Spain to 1537 in Italy. To understand better the vision of La Storta we need to put it in the context of the preceding months, and especially of the early companions' priestly ordination on 24 June 1537. After this had taken place in Venice they dispersed throughout the Veneto region and it fell to Ignatius, Pierre Favre and Diego Laynez to go to Vicenza.

52  *Towards an Understanding of Ignatian Spirituality*

For forty days they devoted themselves to prayer, penance and begging for alms, living the while in extreme poverty. When that phase was over and they had been joined by Jean Codure (1508-1541), all four engaged in public preaching in the city's squares. It is noteworthy that, unlike his companions, Ignatius had postponed celebrating his first Mass, most likely in the increasingly forlorn hope that he could do so in the Holy Land. The *Acta* records:

> During the period that he was in Vicenza, he received many spiritual visions and many rather ordinary consolations (it was just the opposite when he was in Paris), but especially when he began to prepare for his ordination in Venice and when he was getting ready to celebrate Mass. Also during his journeys he enjoyed great supernatural visitations of the kind that he used to have when he was in Manresa [AIP 95].

Note how the relative aridity of Ignatius's prayer during his years of study in Paris is now replaced by more intense spiritual experiences such as he had enjoyed in Manresa. Keeping this in mind, we come to the description of the La Storta vision:

> After he had been ordained a priest, he decided to wait another year before celebrating Mass, preparing himself and praying to our Lady to place him with her Son. One day, a few miles before reaching Rome, while praying in a church, he felt a great change in his soul and so clearly did he see God the Father place him with Christ, his Son, that he had no doubts that God the Father did place him with his Son [AIP 96].

As so often in the *Acta* Ignatius gives the bare details of his experience without any embellishment. But from Favre and Laynez, who were with him, we learn that, as soon as Ignatius entered the small wayside chapel – it was not actually a church – he felt a sudden change come over him.

He sees God the Father, together with Jesus who is carrying his cross. Both Father and Son are looking on him with great kindness,

*Mystical Gifts* 53

and he hears the Father say to the Son, 'I wish you to take this man as your servant'. Jesus then turns and addresses the kneeling pilgrim saying, 'I wish you to be our servant'. Then he hears the Father add, 'I will be favourable to you in Rome'. Whether this promise is to mean success or failure, the fulfilling of his dreams or dreadful persecution, Ignatius is uncertain. But whatever is to happen, he trusts completely that the Lord will be with him. The desire of Ignatius 'to be placed with the Son' echoes the colloquy, or conversational prayer, at the end of the Meditation on Two Standards in the *Spiritual Exercises*. There, the exercitant asks in turn of Mary, the Son and the Father to be

> . . . received under his (Christ's) standard; and first, in the most perfect spiritual poverty; and also, if his Divine Majesty should be served and if he should wish to choose me for it, to no less a degree of actual poverty; and second, in bearing reproaches and injuries, that through them I may imitate him more [147].

On the journey from the north of Italy to Rome, Ignatius is praying for this grace by turning especially to Mary, his intercessor and mother. 'To be placed with the Son' or 'received under his standard' – the phrases are interchangeable – has been a long-standing desire of Ignatius ever since his conversion. Now he is making his petition as a *priest*, however, longing to be placed with the Son so as to share more fully in *his* priesthood. This is why it is so significant that the Christ he sees at La Storta is carrying his cross. He is on his way to Calvary to complete his self-offering to the Father as the High Priest of all creation. Ignatius, now a priest himself, wants to be there with the self-emptying Christ, wants to be one with him. And this is precisely where the Father places him. La Storta is, to a large extent, a manifestation of a priestly spirituality.

Unlike any of his earlier mystical experiences, Ignatius immediately interprets the La Storta vision as intended, not only for himself, but also for all the first companions. This is curious because a mystical experience is always uniquely personal. Besides, only two of these companions are physically present with him in the chapel. It is almost as if Ignatius sees himself as carrying all nine companions in his heart, so that they participate in whatever he is experiencing; or as if this group of friends were already constituted as a 'body', something that did not formally occur until the following year. What is certain is that the other companions too, all recently ordained, are about to offer themselves to the Pope for priestly service anywhere in the world. In Ignatius's mind this would not be happening if they, like himself, had not been placed with Christ carrying his cross. The La Storta vision can be said to reveal the deeper mystique of their companionship which was embedded in their relationship with Christ. It points to the corporate dimension of their calling and of the mission they are soon to receive from the Pope. We will have more to say on this theme.

## Spiritual Diary

From the beginning of his conversion Ignatius had formed the habit of keeping what we might call a spiritual diary or journal. We have seen how the *Spiritual Exercises* grew out of this habit during his stay in Manresa. Throughout his last sixteen years in Rome, he continued to keep a record of his experiences in prayer and his reflections on them. Only part of this later diary has survived, but it helps to enrich our understanding of his mystical gifts. The background is important so we need to describe it here.

In 1541 the composition of constitutions for the recently approved Society of Jesus was entrusted by the early companions to Ignatius and Jean Codure. The latter, however, died within a few months and Ignatius was left alone with the task. The period 1541-1544 turned out to be a time of rapid expansion of the Society. Besides the administrative work involved in governance, Ignatius was engaged in many apostolic projects in Rome itself. All the while he was suffering from serious ill-health. He had little time or energy to give to writing constitutions.

*Mystical Gifts* 55

However, in 1544 there was some easing of work pressures as the Society settled into a period of consolidation. Ignatius took up the composition of constitutions more actively and began to examine the kind of poverty most appropriate for the Society. The central issue was whether a fixed income should be allowed for the sacristies of churches attached to professed houses. He himself had been party to a decision taken by the early companions in 1541 that allowed such an income, but now he had second thoughts and was leaning towards excluding it. So he began a discernment process of forty days which lasted from 2 February until 12 March 1544. What we know as the *Spiritual Diary* dates from this period.[13]

The text, consisting of two fascicules or copybooks, has been helpfully named 'a discernment log-book' by Joseph Munitiz. In it Ignatius, as usual, recorded his inner experiences during prayer. Writing it was an aid to his discernment, just as anyone facing a serious decision today would be helped by making similar notes. Some familiarity with the *Spiritual Exercises*, especially the decision-making process [SE 175-188], is almost essential in order to understand the *Diary's* contents, in particular those in the first copybook.[14] Ignatius also realised that some prayer experiences promised to be of more lasting value and meaning for himself personally, beyond the context of this particular discernment. He noted such passages by encircling them in the manuscript. Later he copied them on to two separate pieces of paper, which have also happily survived.

13. 'The Spiritual Diary' in *Saint Ignatius of Loyola: Personal Writings*, translated with introduction by Joseph A. Munitiz, SJ, and Philip Endean, SJ. London: Penguin Classics (2005). All quotations from the *Diary* will be taken from this translation.

14. Recommended: Timothy M. Gallagher, OMV, *Discerning the Will of God: An Ignatian Guide to Christian Decision Making*. Chestnut Ridge, NY: Crossroad Publishing Company (2010).

56  *Towards an Understanding of Ignatian Spirituality*

Let us turn first to the election, or decision-making process. The answer to the question that Ignatius was posing to himself concerning poverty was not given to him in a self-authenticating illumination, described as a First-Time experience in the *Spiritual Exercises* [175]. So he had to find another approach. He began by composing a separate document, which is likewise extant, noting the pros and cons, as he saw them, of what he was now proposing. He kept these lists by his side during his prayer over this whole period, and there are several references to them in the text of the *Diary* itself. He had clearly opted to use 'the first way of making a good and correct choice' in the Third Time, as outlined in the *Spiritual Exercises* [SE 177-183]. In this way of decision-making, reasoning plays the lead role. But again, this method failed to produce a result with which he could be at peace. So he eventually turned for enlightenment to his experience of consolations and desolations, where affectivity comes more to the fore. In the terminology of the *Exercises*, this is called the Second Time for making a good and sound election [SE 176].[15]

The very difficulties met by Ignatius in this discernment on poverty are part of its value for us. He experienced much uncertainty even about the approach he should take, in discovering the most helpful methodology.[16] His accompanying mystical experiences did not save him from the messiness and confusion that most people know as a feature of discernment. It must be added that few would be as obsessive about getting confirmation of the decision, as unwilling or unable to bring the discernment to a close as Ignatius is here. In this we would do well to ignore his example. However, he got there in the end.

15. There will be more on these Three Times in the next chapter.

16. There is a curious parallel with the *Deliberation of the First Fathers* in 1539 when they too had to change their method of discernment in mid-stream, as it were.

## The Trinity

While the influence of the *Spiritual Exercises* pervades the *Spiritual Diary*, there are new elements in the later mysticism of Ignatius, or at least new emphases. In spite of his vision of the Trinity at Manresa, and what he says about its lasting impression on him, there is little prominence given to the Trinity *as such* in the *Exercises*. The one real exception is the contemplation on the Incarnation [101-109]. Here the image of the Three Persons gazing down on the world and its inhabitants is not only gripping, but it supplies the frame of reference within which the mystery being contemplated unfolds. The striking presence of the Trinity, and its active concern for the world, are essential in releasing the dynamism of this exercise and, through it, that of the entire Second Week. Apart from the Incarnation, however, we are generally left in the *Exercises* with a more implicit, or hidden, presence of the Trinity. This presence is implied in *any* contemplation of Christ, whose relationship with the Father is integral to his identity and who has received an outpouring of the Holy Spirit at his baptism (as Mary had done at his conception).

Similarly, in the Contemplation to Attain Love [230-237], the Trinity can be inferred in a number of ways, most of all from the pervasive theme of mutuality, since the Trinity is a community of mutual love.

This reticence, if such it is, about specifying the Trinity in the *Exercises* is replaced in the *Diary* by a full-blown Trinitarian mysticism. The enlightenments that Ignatius receives vary considerably. He sometimes sees one Person of the Trinity without the others; or the Son and Spirit within the Father; or he may experience the Trinitarian essence without any distinction of persons. As a characteristic example we might consider the final lines he wrote in the first copybook, after finishing his discernment on poverty:

> When I said grace after the meal, the Being of the Father partly disclosed itself, also the Being of the Blessed Trinity, while I felt

58  *Towards an Understanding of Ignatian Spirituality*

> a spiritual impulse moving to devotion and tears, such as I had not felt or seen all day, although I had often sought for it. Today's great visitations had no particular or distinct Person for their object, but in general, the Giver of graces [SD 12 March].

Here, one of the persons, the Father, is made present to him, if only partly, but also the Trinity in itself ('the Being of the Blessed Trinity'). This latter he identifies as 'the Giver of graces'. Joseph Munitiz elegantly explains the connection of this phrase with the Contemplation to Attain Love in the *Exercises*:

> In the *Diary*, an endearing phrase to refer to God is that of 'Giver of graces'; in the Contemplation [to Attain Love], a rough intimation of the treasures these words enclose is imparted. The gift is the Giver himself, a Giver who is both present and dynamic in the gift, a Giver who is infinite in the number and variety of his gifts, to such an extent that no gift is not the Giver himself. Here, in this notion of 'giving', of 'communication', which for Ignatius is the quintessence of love, is to be found the seed, hidden and expectant, of the trinitarian revelations.[17]

## Christ

The centrality of Christ in the *Exercises*, replaced now by that of the Trinity, in no way excludes any reference to Christ. In this entry Ignatius is still deeply moved as he reaffirms his desire to follow Christ:

> While preparing the altar and vesting, the name of Jesus was shown me: I felt great love, confirmation and an increased resolve to follow him. I wept and sobbed. Throughout Mass, very great devotion and many tears so that quite often I lost the

17. *Inigo: Discernment Log-Book. The Spiritual Diary of Saint Ignatius Loyola*, edited and translated by Joseph A. Munitiz, SJ. London: Inigo Enterprises (1987), 13.

power of speech; all the devotion and feelings had Jesus as their object [SD 24 Feb].

Notice that Ignatius does not deliberately choose to contemplate Jesus but that 'the name of Jesus was shown' him. This way of recording his experience is common in the *Diary*. It points to the mystical element in his spirituality at that time. Ignatius is more passive than active, maybe totally passive. If Ignatius is not the active one, however, then who is? One entry in the *Diary* has Ignatius attributing such a revelation of Christ to an intervention of the Trinity:

> It seemed in some way to be from the Blessed Trinity that Jesus was shown or felt, and I remembered the time when the Father put me with the Son [SD 23 Feb].

In the *Exercises* the movement is through Jesus in his humanity to the Father, and so into the life of the Trinity. Here the movement is reversed. It begins from the Trinity, and then continues through Jesus into the mind and heart of Ignatius.

## Holy Spirit

We might also note how in the *Diary* some of the most remarkable visions are of the Third Person. The absence of the Holy Spirit from the pages of the *Exercises* has often been commented on and variously explained. In the *Exercises*, we find a mere five references to the Spirit in the Mysteries of the Life of Christ, where they could hardly be omitted without expurgating the Gospels, and one in the Rules for Thinking with the Church [SE 365]. In contrast, consider the language in the following passage and try imagining what it is attempting to capture:

> A little later I made a colloquy with the Holy Spirit, in preparation for saying his mass; I experienced the same devotion and tears, and seemed to see or feel him in a dense clarity or in the colour of burning flame – a way quite strange to me – all of which confirmed me in my election [SD 11 Feb].

60  *Towards an Understanding of Ignatian Spirituality*

Phrases such as 'a dense clarity' or 'the colour of burning flame' occur frequently in the mystical tradition, but are rare and unexpected in Ignatius. His prose is more usually unadorned and even phlegmatic.

There is an evident dissimilarity, as well as a similarity, between the spirituality of the *Exercises* and that of the *Diary*. Some may prefer to speak of continuity and discontinuity. It is not a totally new spirituality that emerges in the *Diary*, but one that has evolved considerably from that of the *Exercises* and the Manresa experiences that underpinned them. Peak experiences have become more frequent, if not the norm. The unitive dimension of prayer is predominant. Taking everything into account, the *Spiritual Diary* offers the strongest evidence for regarding Ignatius as one of the great Christian mystics.

*chapter five*

# Discernment in the Tradition

Most of the elements of discernment were present in the Judeo-Christian tradition well before Ignatius. He learned about them through his reading at Loyola and his theological studies at the University of Paris. All of this acquired knowledge, however, was subsidiary to the wisdom that he gained by attending to what was happening within himself. This combination of inner experience and academic learning was to be embedded later in Jesuit formation. Learning on its own remains objective and theoretical, but inner experience is frequently, if not always, ambiguous. Learning needs inner experience to ground and validate it, while experience requires a language and methodology to articulate and interpret it. An interaction or collaboration between the two is essential. However, Ignatius not only had roots in, and relied on, an inherited wisdom, but he contributed to its further development. So much so that what we now call Ignatian spirituality is often identified with discernment. This claim can at times be exaggerated (especially when other Christian sources are ignored), yet it does express an important truth.

What, then, was his contribution? Was there something new or different in the way that he understood the ancient teaching?

Two points can be made.

Firstly, Ignatius was a skilled pedagogue. He found ways, particularly in the *Exercises* and is his letters, to alert or sensitise people to the reality of the spirits – good and evil – whose presence in

## 62   Towards an Understanding of Ignatian Spirituality

human lives called for discernment. Then he expertly taught methods of interpreting and dealing with these spirits. He managed to simplify the traditional teaching without ever being simplistic.

Secondly, Ignatius detected how the discernment of spirits, as elucidated in the tradition, could be put at the service of decision-making. No one before him had made this link so explicitly or described in such detail the process it involved.

All serious decision-making requires discernment of spirits, but not all discernment of spirits leads necessarily to decision-making. Teasing out such ideas was innovative.

## Communication with the Divine

It will be helpful to touch upon ways in which God, or the Divine, has been understood to communicate with human beings, and human beings with God. This is obviously a central area of interest for understanding discernment. In this outline we include non-Christian and even non-religious sources, such as philosophy. In general, humans have looked to three different modes of divine communication: the paranormal, reason and affectivity.[18]

### Paranormal

In the *Apologia* of Plato (427-347 BC) Socrates, who is being tried for blasphemy against the gods of the state, is speaking in his own defence. The particular issue at this point in his speech is his refusal to enter politics. He says:

> It may seem curious that I should go round giving advice like this and busying myself in people's private affairs, and yet never venture publicly to address you as a whole and advise on matters

---

18. This section is indebted to the important article by Michael J. Buckley, SJ, entitled 'The Structure of the Rules for Discernment', in Philip Sheldrake (editor), *The Way of Ignatius Loyola: Contemporary Approaches to the Spiritual Exercises*. London: SPCK (1991), 219-237.

of state. The reason for this is what you have often heard me say before on many other occasions: that I am subject to a divine or supernatural experience, which Meletus saw fit to travesty in his indictment. It began in my early childhood – a sort of voice which comes to me; and when it comes it always dissuades me from what I am proposing to do, and never urges me on. It is this that debars me from entering public life [31d].[19]

Some have suggested that Socrates is simply referring to his conscience, but the background of the whole discussion points to a mysterious source outside of himself ('I am subject to'), which he describes as 'divine or supernatural' (sometimes translated 'divine or daimonic'). This corresponds more to what we mean by the paranormal.

Other examples could include the Christian, Jewish and Muslim belief in angels, who are a source of enlightenment and providence for humankind. Mystical texts such as the *Kabbalah* posit an archetypal world which functions as a source of mediation between the divine and the human. In less overtly philosophical or religious movements one can point to the Astral Plane among devotees of the occult, to the ghosts of the dead in the teaching of the Spiritualists, and to the movement of the stars as revelatory for astrologers.

### Reason

The second mode of divine communication is through human reason. In this context reason strives to breach the limitations and opacity of the material world and of mere sensory knowledge. It seeks to arrive at the transcendent which is a realm far above and beyond us. This movement of reason is most often described in terms of an ascent. We climb upward, as if by a series of steps, to

---

19. Plato, *The Last Days of Socrates: Euthyphro – Apology – Crito – Phaedo,* translated by Hugh Tredennick and Harold Tarrant. London: Penguin Books (revised 1993), 58.

64  *Towards an Understanding of Ignatian Spirituality*

reach the transcendent realm. There the divine communicates with us, and we with the divine.

Plato held that reasoning and learning are interrelated. There is a continuity between one kind of knowledge, or one level of discovery, and another. Having pursued the true and the beautiful in an upward movement through all the disciplines, reason reaches its final fulfilment. This is the contemplation of that which is best in existence, the Supreme Good (*Republic*, VII, 532-534). Some centuries later Plotinus (c. AD 204-270), the founder of Neo-Platonism, wrote:

> Things here are signs, they show therefore to the wiser teachers how the supreme God may be known; the instructed priest reading the sign may enter the holy place and make real the vision of the inaccessible (Enneads, VI, 9, 11).[20]

For Plotinus the goal is attained, and the search culminates, in vision and ecstasy. But the path traversed, and the guidance a person receives throughout the journey, is the dispassionate use of the mind and reason. Years of serious human thought, given to 'reading the sign', are required before entering 'the holy place'.

When we come to the Christian tradition, we find the Jesuit theologian, polemicist and cardinal, St Robert Bellarmine (1542-1621), writing a major work entitled *The Mind's Ascent to God by a Ladder of Created Things*.[21] In Bellarmine's argumentation we see that the Platonic paradigm is alive and well: the notion of an ascent, the image of a ladder or steps, the created world providing data for our reasoning, the interrelatedness of truths, and the journey's end being God.

---

20. Plotinus, *The Enneads*, translated by Stephen McKenna. New York: Larson Publications (1993).

21. St. Robert Bellarmine, *The Mind's Ascent to God by a Ladder of Created Things*, in *Robert Bellarmine, Spiritual Writings*, translated by John Patrick Donnelly, SJ, and Roland J. Teske, SJ. New York/Mahwah: Paulist Press (1988), 51-225.

This kind of intellectual mysticism, if we may so call it, also underlies the coherence that is frequently asserted between the religious and scientific consciousness. We recognise it in scholars such as the mathematician and astronomer Johannes Kepler (1571-1630), the palaeontologist Teilhard de Chardin, SJ (1881-1955), and ecological theologians such as Thomas Berry (1914-2008). Far from being led into atheism, or even agnosticism, these scientists view their research as unveiling the mystery and majesty of God, and as bringing them into deeper union with God, the One who is Ever Greater.

## Affectivity

The claims of writers such as Bellarmine and others for the supremacy, indeed the uniqueness, of reason in our search for God have often been challenged. Affectivity, feelings or emotions are appealed to instead by those who consider reason an inadequate vehicle for attaining to God. The following are some widely known quotations that illustrate this conviction.

- 'By love he (God) may be sought and held, but by thinking never', says the anonymous author of *The Cloud of Unknowing*, writing in the late fourteenth century. Note how stark a contrast this statement sets up with the views of writers such as Bellarmine.

- 'I would rather feel compunction of heart for my sins than merely know the definition of compunction', says Thomas à Kempis (1380-1471) in *The Imitation of Christ*. This classic spiritual manual was a constant companion for Ignatius and, apart from the Bible, is the only book he recommends to the retreatant in the *Spiritual Exercises*.

- 'The heart has its reasons which reason does not know', writes Blaise Pascal (1623-1662) in his *Pensées*. This aphorism is all the more striking coming from an intellectual genius such as Pascal.

## 66   *Towards an Understanding of Ignatian Spirituality*

One of the most stimulating writers on the importance of feelings is John Wesley (1703-1791), the founder of Methodism. He left voluminous writings of which the most personal is his *Journal*.[22] Often quoted is the description of a conversion experience that was certainly important for him at the time, a stepping stone on his life's journey.

> In the evening, I went very unwillingly to a society in Aldersgate Street, where one was reading Luther's preface to the Epistle to the Romans. About a quarter before nine, while he was describing the change which God works in the heart through faith in Christ, I felt my heart strangely warmed. I felt I did trust in Christ, Christ alone for salvation; and an assurance was given me that he had taken away my sins, even mine, and saved me from the law of sin and death (24 May 1728).

This passage records how Wesley moved from a notional acceptance of the salvation brought by Christ to a deeply personal one (*'my* sins, even *mine'*). This change was brought about by feelings ('my heart strangely warmed') and led to 'assurance'. In a later *Journal* entry he writes:

> For a Christian is one who has the fruits of the Spirit of Christ, which (to mention no more) are love, peace, joy. But these I have not. I have not any love of God. I do not love either the Father or the Son. Do you ask how do I know whether I love God? I answer by another question, 'How do you know whether you love me?' Why, as you know whether you are hot or cold. You feel at this moment that you do or do not love me. And I feel at this moment that I do not love God, which therefore I know because I feel it (4 January 1739).

---

22. *The Journal of the Rev. John Wesley AM,* 8 volumes, edited by Nehemiah Curnock. London: The Epworth Press (1960 reprint).

This is one of the strongest affirmations in the Christian tradition of the crucial role played by feelings. Wesley was consistent in this teaching, as in a much later *Journal* entry we read:

> The very thing which Mr Stinstra calls fanaticism is no other than heart-religion; in other words, 'righteousness, and peace, and joy in the Holy Ghost'. These must be felt, or they have no being. All therefore who condemn inward feelings in the gross, leave no place either for joy or peace or love in religion, and consequently reduce it to a dry, dead carcass (12 August 1771).

At the risk of exaggerating somewhat, we might say that if Bellarmine is all head, Wesley is all heart.

### Coda

It can be shown that Ignatius is open to all three of these modes of mutual communication with God – paranormal, reason, affectivity – when he deals with discernment in the *Exercises*. One might reflect in a particular way on how they correspond to the Three Times for making an election [175-177], referred to in the last chapter when discussing the *Spiritual Diary*. The correspondence is not total but it is enough to be significant.

## Old Testament

Looking into the biblical tradition, we begin with the Old Testament. None of its writings offers any systematic treatment of discernment, but it was certainly practised among the Hebrews. We have to abstract their understanding of what they were doing from the stories that they tell. The Old Testament contains an abundance of material describing how individuals, and indeed the whole community of Israel, were called to make serious choices in the course of their lives. In these they sought to do the will of God and they trusted in his guidance. They were aware, however, that other influences were also at play in their hearts. Human

68 *Towards an Understanding of Ignatian Spirituality*

beings were prone to be deceived under the appearance of the good, of a seductive but illusory promise. As Eve said to God in the Garden of Eden, 'The serpent tricked me, and I ate' (Gen 3:13).

Good and evil spirits were said to come upon a human being. All these spirits remained under the dominion of God but they led a person in opposite directions.

> Now the spirit of the Lord departed from Saul, and an evil spirit from the Lord tormented him. And Saul's servants said to him, 'See now, an evil spirit from God is tormenting you' (1 Sam 16:14-15).

The Hebrews were more comfortable than we are with the idea of an evil spirit coming from God. A Christian writer would probably prefer to say that God allowed an evil spirit to harass Saul. In both cases God's sovereignty is preserved. Nothing happens outside of his will.

Ignatius is surprisingly reticent about the source or origin of the evil spirits. He concentrates instead on what they do and on the tactics they employ. As so often, his is a practical rather than a speculative theology. 'But just as the good spirit is chiefly the one who guides and counsels us in time of consolation, so it is the evil spirit who does this in time of desolation' [SE 318]. Consider also the colourful descriptions of how the 'enemy', as he sometimes calls the evil spirit, attacks and manipulates us [SE 325-327].

But Old Testament writers do not always attribute inner turmoil, seductive temptations, or deceptive advice to an evil spirit. They have enough psychological awareness and acumen to recognise that the human heart itself is a source of enormous ambivalence. 'The heart is devious above all else; it is perverse – who can understand it?' (Jer 17:9).

### True and False Prophecy
The prophets saw themselves as called by God to assert his presence and mediate his decrees to the people, especially to their leaders.

*Discernment in the Tradition* 69

But how test the authenticity of a prophet and his utterances? Criteria were needed, and over time they began to be formulated. The first appeared as far back as the book of Deuteronomy where Moses is anticipating the later appearance of the great prophets.

> You may say to yourself, 'How can we recognise a word that the Lord has not spoken?' If a prophet speaks in the name of the Lord but the thing does not take place or prove true, it is a word that the Lord has not spoken. The prophet has spoken it presumptuously; do not be frightened by it (Deut 18:21-22).

This criterion may strike us as simplistic and not much use in a time of crisis. If a prophet announces the fall of our city to the enemy, do we have to wait until the catastrophe happens before we flee to safety? That will be too late. Linked with this criterion is another which holds that a prophecy of misfortune is normally authentic, but a prophecy of good fortune is authentic only when it is verified by the event (Jer 28:8-9). This criterion may also seem rather crude.

Other criteria emerged, however, as Israel gained more experience of prophecy and learned more nuanced ways of interpretation. Among them are the following:

- A prophet's orthodoxy, or identification with the faith of Israel, must be apparent. Even if some dramatic event happens in line with a prophet's words, this will not guarantee that he is sent by God if his faith is unorthodox.

- A prophet's moral behaviour must also be considered. See the long passage in which false prophets are denounced, mostly on grounds of their immorality (Jer 23:9-40).

- Of a similar nature is the criterion of the prophet's intention or motivation. Is he genuinely free or, for example, is he beholden to the king? Does he have some vested interest in having his message believed?

70  *Towards an Understanding of Ignatian Spirituality*

- The prophets themselves present their personal experience as the ultimate justification of the word they speak. This is why so many of them deem it essential to give an account of their call from God (Am 7:14-15; Hos 1-3; Jer 1; Ezek 1-3).

## New Testament

The main addition that the New Testament brings to the subject of discernment is its elaborated teaching on the Holy Spirit. Paul taught that one of the gifts of the Spirit, freely given to some believers, is precisely the discernment of spirits.

> Now there are varieties of gifts . . . To one is given through the Spirit the utterance of wisdom, and to another the utterance of knowledge according to the same Spirit, to another faith by the same Spirit, to another gifts of healing by the one Spirit, to another the working of miracles, to another prophecy, to another the discernment of spirits . . . (1 Cor 12:4, 9-10).

In Greek this last gift is called *diakrisis pneumaton*, and in Latin translation *discretio spirituum*. This is the terminology that we have inherited and that has served us well. But even in the earliest document in the New Testament, before the terminology became established, we read, 'Do not quench the Spirit. Do not despise the words of prophets, but test everything' (1 Thess 5:19-21). That already describes discernment in a nutshell. And in one of the later documents, we read, 'Beloved, do not believe every spirit, but test the spirits to see whether they are from God; for many false prophets have gone out into the world' (1 Jn 4:1).

## New Testament Criteria

As in the Old Testament, various criteria are proposed to aid in discernment. Most occur in the writings of Paul. Some examples:

- Good and evil spirits are to be recognised by their fruits.

*Discernment in the Tradition* 71

- The opposition is not just between good and evil spirits as such, but between the desires and fruits of the Holy Spirit and the desires and fruits of the flesh.

- The authentic gifts of the Spirit are those that serve the common good (1 Cor 12:7); build up the Church (1 Cor 14:4); and contribute to the unity of the body of Christ (Eph 4:4-6)

- The Holy Spirit shows its presence by powerful signs: miracles, confidence in communicating God's word, and dealing joyfully with persecutions.

Our message of the gospel came to you not in word only, but also in power and in the Holy Spirit and with full conviction; just as you know what kind of persons we proved to be among you for your sake. And you became imitators of us and of the Lord, for in spite of persecution you received the word with joy inspired by the Holy Spirit (1 Thess 1:4-6).

- Among these potent signs, God's direct communication with a prophet or apostle is fundamental. In Paul's own case, the vision on the road to Damascus gives him the assurance of being called, set apart, and sent to proclaim the Risen Lord among the Gentiles (Rom 1:1; Gal 1:15-16; Phil 3:12).

- Genuine gifts are marked by light and peace. They are not blind impulses that stir up discord and commotion (1 Cor 14:32-33; 2 Cor 7:10). Notice the connection of this criterion to the many contrasts that Ignatius draws in the *Exercises* between the activity of good and evil spirits:

In those progressing from good to better . . . it is characteristic of the evil spirit to cause gnawing anxiety, to sadden, and to set up obstacles. In this way he unsettles these persons by false reasons aimed at preventing their progress; but . . . it is characteristic of the good spirit to stir up courage and strength, consolations, tears, inspirations and tranquillity. He makes

## 72  *Towards an Understanding of Ignatian Spirituality*

things easier and eliminates all obstacles, so that the persons may move forward in doing good [SE 315].

- Charity is not only an unchanging sign of the Spirit in a community or an individual. It becomes a guiding principle that works within discernment (Phil 1:9; Eph 4:14-15).

- Perhaps the supreme criterion of discernment for Paul, as for the evangelists, is a person's attitude towards Christ. 'No one can say "Jesus is Lord" except by the Holy Spirit' (1 Cor 12:3). The Holy Spirit is certainly present in a person who makes this act of faith.

As with the Old Testament, there is no systematic theology of discernment in the New. Still less do its authors leave us a handbook for discernment, as Ignatius would do in the *Spiritual Exercises*. Nevertheless, in describing the life of the early Christians, the New Testament shows how embedded the practice of discernment is among them. This is mainly because they are so conscious of the active presence of the Holy Spirit in their communities. Perhaps the contemporary challenge is to recover that same awareness of the Spirit at work in ourselves and in today's world. Only then will Ignatius's rules and guidelines be effective.

### Wisdom of the Desert

Not long after New Testament times some Christians, for reasons which are still in dispute, moved out of the cities and towns of the Roman Empire and took up residence in the deserts – the harsh, infertile, intimidating wilderness areas of Palestine, Syria and Egypt. This began as a trickle as early as the second century, but it gained momentum from the later third century onwards. The generic word to describe these men and women – among whom men were a significant majority – was *ascetics*. The first individuals tended to live as solitaries or anchorites. Among these the Abba

Antony (251-356) was the best known and most influential. However, the majority chose to live as cenobites, that is in community. Abba Pachomius (292-348), Antony's near contemporary, was the first great monastic legislator. Both styles of living, anchoritic and cenobitic, were the soil in which what became known as the Wisdom of Desert grew and flourished. At the heart of this wisdom was discernment of spirits.

The preliminary step in unlocking this wisdom is to understand the double symbolism of the desert in the Bible. On the one hand, the desert is the place where a people, or an individual, meets God, especially in a time of crisis. Crossing the desert during the Exodus, as they escaped from slavery in Egypt, the Hebrews knew that they had found favour with God. This is sometimes called the honeymoon period of their mutual relationship, both because of the heightened awareness of God's closeness to them, and the delight that they took in this intimacy. On the other hand, the desert has a darker, more sinister symbolic meaning. It is the natural habitat of the evil spirits, hence a location where spiritual combat becomes inevitable. Those who go into the desert are deliberately engaging with the demons on their own home territory. They are invading their homeland, where the fighting can be expected to be face to face and ferocious.

Life in the desert can, with caution, be seen as a kind of controlled laboratory experiment. There, without the supports of ordinary living, the human spirit is exposed in its nakedness to the powerful influence of both good and evil spirits. It finds itself caught up in their cosmic struggle for supremacy. Note how Ignatius recreates, while also adapting, this desert scenario in his introductory notes to the *Exercises*. He presents it as the most suitable context for engaging with God and receiving the graces of the Exercises:

> Ordinarily, in making these (exercises) an exercitant will achieve more progress the more he or she withdraws from all friends and acquaintances, and from all earthly concerns; for example,

## 74    *Towards an Understanding of Ignatian Spirituality*

by moving out of one's place of residence and taking a different house or room where one can live in the greatest possible solitude [SE 20].

Because of the isolation and harshness of life in the desert, and of being drawn into a spiritual combat that was beyond their control, some casualties inevitably occurred among the ascetics. Some suffered mental illnesses of one kind or another, emotional breakdowns and even, in extreme cases, madness. This was a particular risk among those who were new to this way of life, or unprepared for it physically, psychologically or spiritually.

To avoid such casualties the need for guidance was acute. Accordingly, newcomers to the desert were encouraged to seek out an elder, an 'abba' or 'amma', who had already been seasoned by solitude and so possessed an experiential knowledge of the spirits and of the life of prayer. A key phrase in the desert tradition was the request, 'Give me a word'. This was addressed to one's abba or amma. The 'word' sought was not simply an explanation or an instruction, still less a general maxim. It was seen as a word of life, unique to each individual in their specific situation. Its main purpose was to reveal and heal particular weaknesses or deficiencies in the seeker. This 'word' was not to be discussed or analysed or disputed in any way. At times it might be obscure, or apparently contradictory, even unintelligible to the rational mind – somewhat like a Zen koan.

It is important to stress that these 'words' (Greek: *apophthegmata*) were never intended for anyone except the monk who sought for help. However, the temptation to treat them as general maxims inevitably arose when they were collected and circulated.[23] These collections, however useful in giving a glimpse of the kind of dialogue that took place between the elder and the person seeking guidance, risk distorting the oral tradition. This was based

---

23. These *apophthegmata* were gathered into three collections: the *Alphabetical Collection*, the *Anonymous Collection*, and the *Systematic Collection*.

on the unique relationship between two individuals: the elder and the disciple. Such a model has continued ever since – with variations – in the relationship between spiritual director and directee and, in the Ignatian tradition, that between the one who gives and the one who makes the Spiritual Exercises.

## Other Sources

Another important source for this desert tradition of discernment is the *Life of Antony* by St Athanasius of Alexandria.[24] Antony (251-356), whom we have already mentioned, was a friend of Athanasius, although their personalities and life experience could hardly have been more dissimilar. One was a hermit or solitary, seeking God directly through spiritual experience and ascetic discipline, retiring deeper and deeper into the Egyptian desert, the other was not only bishop of a major cosmopolitan see in the Mediterranean world, but a learned and sophisticated theologian. Antony belonged to the oral tradition of the desert; Athanasius was a product of the literary tradition from which emerged the writings of the great Fathers of the Church. But in spite of these differences the two men shared a mutual respect and warmth. The *Life*, with its vivid and sometimes lurid stories of the temptations endured by Antony, teaches us much about discernment as practised by one of its acknowledged experts.

So far we have been dealing mainly with the experiential side of discernment. But, as always happens, experience that is reflected on over decades, and even centuries, eventually produces theology. Origin (185-254) was one of the first to reflect on the desert tradition from a theological perspective, but the real master of this genre was Evagrius of Pontus (345-399). Later, and indebted to Evagrius, was the influential John Climacus (579-649) who treats of discernment in his *Ladder of Divine Ascent*. Like the desert

---

24. Athanasius, *The Life of Antony and the Letter to Marcellinus*, translated by Robert C. Gregg. New York/Mahwah: Paulist Press (1979).

## 76 *Towards an Understanding of Ignatian Spirituality*

experiment itself, these three writers belong to eastern Christianity. It took another monk-theologian to transplant this tradition to the west.

John Cassian (360-442) had lived in Egypt for some years and had met all of the abbas who were regarded as experts in the spiritual life. He then set up a monastery in Marseilles which was based on the Egyptian model. His greatest work, known as the *Conferences*, consists of twenty-four long interviews with the monks he had come to know in Egypt. The conferences are most likely expansions of what these masters had actually said to him. Discernment of spirits is a topic that is implicitly present in all the conferences but it is highlighted in a fuller, more explicit way in the Second Conference, based on a conversation with the Abba Moses. After his death, Cassian continued to mediate the Wisdom of the Desert, through his writings, to succeeding generations of Christians – Ignatius included. And Ignatius has mediated it to us.

*chapter six*

# Personal and Corporate

This book has the term 'Ignatian Spirituality' in its subtitle. So far we have been consistent in using it, as indeed have most contemporary writers on the subject. Forty or fifty years ago, however, we would probably have written about 'Jesuit Spirituality'. Why the change? Are the terms Jesuit and Ignatian not synonymous? Or can we distinguish between the two? And if we can, does the distinction matter? Are we merely playing with words or is something more substantial involved?

## Life Revisited

To answer these questions it will help to return to Ignatius's life. Up to their priestly ordination, he and his companions were laymen. As students in Paris they had been living a spirituality that was grounded in the *Spiritual Exercises*. They sought to discover the will of God regarding their future. By 1534 they felt ready to commit themselves to the service of God by making vows of poverty and chastity. They also vowed to go on pilgrimage to the Holy Land, but they had added a rider: if they were unable to get to the Holy Land they would travel instead to Rome and make themselves available to the pope.

Their foresight proved to be prudent but also providential. When the time came for their intended voyage across the Mediterranean, war between Venice and the Turks prevented all pilgrim

78  *Towards an Understanding of Ignatian Spirituality*

ships from sailing. So the rider came into effect and the companions, all now ordained, headed for Rome. The Pope readily accepted their offer of availability, and he soon began to act on it by sending them on missions.

The first of these were within Italy but the companions knew that eventually they would be dispersed more widely. It was imperative that they deal with this new situation and so they entered on a process of discernment. This is recorded in a document known as the *Deliberation of the First Fathers*. At the end of this discernment they had decided to strengthen the bonds already existing between them by forming a new religious order.

In this way the Society of Jesus, soon to be known as the Jesuits, came into being. Ignatius was elected its first superior general and was commissioned to write constitutions for the new order. As well as being a juridical document, the *Constitutions* he wrote needed to give expression to a specifically Jesuit spirituality – a spirituality for a body of men living under vows in the service of the Church.

Is the distinction between Ignatian and Jesuit spirituality beginning to emerge? The first companions lived Ignatian spirituality up to the moment when they became a religious order. For most of that time they were laymen, for a short period they were secular priests. Once they made religious vows, however, they began to live Jesuit spirituality. They did not cease to live Ignatian spirituality, and continued to find their inspiration in the *Exercises*. But these were now subsumed by their Jesuit *Constitutions*.[25]

## Individualistic?

Critics have sometimes indicted Ignatian spirituality with being individualistic. They accuse it of focusing entirely on the needs of the person, while ignoring the corporate dimension of human life. There are many ways of answering such criticism, such as empha-

25. Saint Ignatius of Loyola, *The Constitutions of the Society of Jesus*, translated with an Introduction and Commentary by George E. Ganss, SJ. St. Louis, MO: Institute of Jesuit Sources (1970).

sising that an individual only becomes a person through relationships. To help an individual person is to help all those with whom they associate, who make up their world. One can also point out that Ignatian spirituality encourages the person to be outward looking and engaged with society. It is certainly not a withdrawal from, or apathy in face of the world and its exigent needs.

During his time in Manresa, Ignatius moved from seeking personal perfection through asceticism to seeking 'to help souls' through service. He soon realised that one person alone could achieve relatively little even over a lifetime of dedication. But imagine if that person were part of a group and all its members shared a commitment to a life of service! How much more good could they do! So quite early on, Ignatius tried to attract companions to join him in Spain. These efforts ultimately failed, but he renewed his efforts later at the University of Paris with considerably more success.

What was happening through these developments can be described as a movement *from the personal to the corporate*. It was a gradual change that was later explored and tested by the companions in Paris. At the start, theirs was an informal grouping of 'friends in the Lord' – a term used by Ignatius in one of his letters – which was to some extent provisional, and had no legal status. This changed in 1540 with the establishment of the Society of Jesus.

The *Constitutions* gave expression to this new corporate reality, not only in juridical terms, but by articulating a corresponding corporate spirituality to give it a heart. What was happening can be envisaged as a shift from a personal spirituality based on the Exercises (but with corporate implications) to a corporate spirituality based on the *Constitutions* (but encompassing the personal). In other words, from Ignatian to Jesuit spirituality.

## Exercises and Constitutions

The Spiritual Exercises are available to everyone who is likely to profit from making them, whether in their entirety or in one of their many modified forms. The *Constitutions*, in contrast, were

80  *Towards an Understanding of Ignatian Spirituality*

written for, and directly concern, Jesuits. This last statement needs to be nuanced, however. Experience has shown that many people outside the Society can benefit from the teaching of the *Constitutions* on particular issues. For example, its ways of discussing mission and ministry can be enlightening for those lay or ordained Christians who offer service, remunerated or voluntary, within the Church.

More generally still, the *Constitutions* can be a resource for any group wishing to apply Ignatian spirituality within its corporate context. Examples include family, workplace, professional association, parish community, voluntary body and political organisation. The Exercises remain foundational, but on their own may not be sufficient since they lack an overtly corporate dimension. But the corporate ethos of the *Constitutions* presents a pattern that can be adapted by any group that seeks to find God *as a group*, and not just as a collection of individuals.

One of the greatest challenges for any such group is when decisions have to be made about controversial matters. At times these may even touch on the identity or goals of the group itself, its self-understanding. Such decision-making can either shatter the cohesion of a group or – sometimes paradoxically – strengthen and reaffirm its unity. The *Constitutions* have much to say about creating and strengthening a union of minds and hearts in day-to-day life, as well as during times of decision-making or even of crisis.

## Deliberation of the First Fathers

It must be admitted that the *Constitutions* is a difficult work to understand. Hence, using it outside the Society of Jesus requires expert guidance and mentoring. On a more accessible level, however, there is also much to be learned from the way in which Ignatius and his first companions went about deciding their future in 1539. We have already referred to *The Deliberation of the First Fathers*, the document that officially records the discernment process involved. This has the advantage of being less complicated than the *Constitutions*. While technically it does not contain the minutes of these

*Personal and Corporate* 81

meetings, nevertheless it has something akin to the immediacy of minutes. The document provides an enlightening template for corporate decision-making and is much invoked in Ignatian circles today.[26] For this reason we will give it some attention.

The companions do not gather for this deliberation in order to reopen the whole question of what God wanted them to do with their lives. They already had certain basic convictions, based on their own spiritual experience – personal and corporate – over many years, as well as on the Pope's acceptance of their availability. We see these certainties expressed in the opening paragraph of the text of the *Deliberation*:

> With Lent drawing to a close, as the time was approaching for us to be scattered and parted from one another (something we were eagerly anticipating so that we could the sooner achieve our appointed goal on which we had set our minds and hearts), we resolved to get together for a good long time before our dispersal, and to discuss our vocation and covenanted way of life [D 1].

Their goal, the purpose and orientation of their lives, is clear to them. The deliberation is to be about means, not ends. It is as if they are saying, 'Given all that has happened, how do we reach our goal in these new circumstances when the Pope is scattering us to different places and we can no longer remain together?' Note the question, 'How do we reach our goal?' – not 'What is our goal?'

## Differences Rooted in Nationalities

In the same opening paragraph the text outlines some of the difficulties facing the companions in their decision-making.

---

26. 'The Deliberation that Started the Jesuits', translated with commentary by Jules Toner, SJ, *Studies in the Spirituality of Jesuits*, 6/4 (1974). Quotations from the text will be taken from this translation. References will use the conventional paragraph numbering (as in Toner).

82  *Towards an Understanding of Ignatian Spirituality*

> Some of us were French, others Spanish, Savoyards, or Canta-
> brians. After meeting for many sessions, there was a cleavage
> of sentiments and opinions about our situation. While we all
> had one mind and heart in seeking God's gracious and perfect
> will according to the scope of our vocation; nevertheless, regard-
> ing the more readily effective and more fruitful ways of achiev-
> ing God's will for ourselves and others, we held diverse views
> . . . Since we did hold different judgements, we were eagerly
> on the watch to discover some unobstructed way along which
> we might advance together and all of us offer ourselves as a
> holocaust to our God, in whose praise, honour and glory we
> would yield our all. At last we made a decision [D 1].

From its beginnings at the University of Paris the group around
Ignatius was international in its composition. Initially this may
have come about simply due to circumstances. Later, however,
internationalism became one of the main hallmarks of the Society
of Jesus, a central part of its ideology, and an expression of the
global vision of Ignatius and his co-founders. The benefits, they
realised, were enormous; the price – well worth paying – was to
accept the inevitable clash of temperaments and perspectives between different nationalities.

## A Way Forward

In the *Deliberation*, the 'unobstructed way', which they saw as necessary, is shown to have two dimensions: prayer and discussion.

> In full agreement we settled on this: that we would give ourselves
> to prayer, Masses and meditations more fervently than usual
> and, after doing our very best, we would for the rest cast all our
> concerns on the Lord, hoping in him. He is so kind and generous
> that he never denies his good Spirit to anyone who petitions
> him in humility and simplicity of heart; rather, he gives to all
> generously (Jas 1:5), not holding back from anyone. In no way

then would he, who is kindness itself, desert us; rather he would be with us more generously than we asked or imagined [D 1].

'We will give ourselves to prayer' is the central statement in this passage. But there is much more. The inner attitudes of the companions are spelled out. Taken together they generate an atmosphere permeated by faith and hope. We recognise here the Ignatian polarity between the divine and the human. The companions will do their very best, but at the same time they will 'cast all our concerns on the Lord, hoping in him'. Human effort will be called for and generously given, but on its own it will never be sufficient.

The companions are acutely aware that for true and fruitful discernment the Holy Spirit is needed. They are totally convinced, however, that God always gives his Spirit to those who ask 'in humility and simplicity of heart'. The text piles phrase upon phrase to underline the trust and confidence that the companions have in God's help. God will not look benignly on their efforts from afar, but will be labouring with them. He will gift them with enlightenment to understand and courage to decide. Such are their presuppositions, without which their discernment would not reveal God's will to them, and so would not be fruitful.

## Daily Routine

The text then describes what a typical day was like at this early stage of the discernment:

> We began, therefore, to expend every human effort. We proposed to ourselves some questions worthy of careful consideration and forethought at this opportune time. Throughout the day, we were accustomed to ponder and meditate on these and to prayerfully search into them. At night each one shared with the group what he judged to be more appropriate and helpful with the intention that all with one mind would embrace the

84  *Towards an Understanding of Ignatian Spirituality*

truer way of thinking, tested and commended by the more powerful reasons and by majority vote [D 2].

This segment gives us the first portrayal of the corporate discernment process itself. It is far from complex. The companions are to pray on the issues throughout the day – presumably along with their pastoral ministries – and to gather in the evening to share and discuss. No particular method of sharing is proposed. A certain informality is implied. The stress is on a reasoned approach to the questions they are facing. The companions are not demanding consensus but will accept the view of the majority. Later they will discover that this particular procedure is not always adequate. It will function for non-controversial issues but will run into trouble when topics become potentially divisive. This is the model they use as they begin the deliberation.

## First 5: Union

Two main questions surface for the companions in 1539. The first concerns the future of their relationships with each other in light of their new circumstances. They realise that the casual 'friends in the Lord' paradigm will no longer meet their requirements. This had served them quite satisfactorily while they were studying together in Paris, but it did not fit the new reality of being sent to different places, individually or in small groups, by the pope. The text expresses their predicament very clearly.

> Given that we had offered and dedicated ourselves and our lives to Christ Our Lord and to his true and legitimate Vicar on earth, so that he might dispose of us and send us wherever he judged it to be more fruitful, whether to the Turks or to the Indies or to heretics or to others of the faithful or pagans, would it, or would it not, be more advantageous for our purpose to be so joined and bound together in one body that no physical distance, no matter how great, would separate us? [D 3].

The question has now been formulated. We notice the first appearance of the word 'body' that will later be a key concept in the *Constitutions*. This term is not unrelated to the internationalism of the Society, but it owes most to Paul's teaching on the body of Christ (1 Cor 12:12-31; Eph 4:1-16). In the context of the *Deliberation*, 'body' denotes a more formal, and more organic, structure than the informality of 'friends in the Lord'. The companions could have chosen to remain as un-incardinated secular priests – that is, priests who are not tied to any particular diocese – but totally available to the pope for worldwide missions. This arrangement could have been negotiated on an individual basis, without any correlation with the other companions. Alternatively, they could find some way of remaining bound to each other. This is the option they choose:

> In the end we established the affirmative answer to this question, i.e. that in as much as our most kind and affectionate Lord has deigned to gather us together and unite us, men so spiritually weak and from such diverse geographical and cultural backgrounds, we ought day by day to strengthen and stabilise our union, rendering ourselves one body with special concern for each other, in order to effect the greater spiritual good of our fellow men [D 3].

Their companionship and friendship are God's gift to them, to be treasured and fostered. They would be spurning this gift if they decided to go each his own way. So their friendship will be carefully preserved. The companions also realise, however, that this gift of friendship has not been given to them simply to enjoy but to tap into as a vibrant source of apostolic energy.

## Second Question: Kind of Union

This first decision leads to a further question: what kind of union do they want? Becoming a religious order is one conceivable way forward but there is no unanimity around it. The companions do

86　*Towards an Understanding of Ignatian Spirituality*

not know if that is God's will. However, they formulate their second question around this possibility. In doing so they are not prejudging the issue but giving their discernment a concrete focus. We notice how simple they keep the question. There is no alternative proposed. They are not asking themselves to choose between possibility A and possibility B; the option is between possibility A and possibility not-A. If they choose not-A the question will have to be reformulated and the discernment process will begin again.

> All of us had already pronounced a vow of perpetual chastity and a vow of poverty . . . The question now was this: would it be advantageous to pronounce a third vow, viz. of obedience to someone from among us in order that we might more sincerely and with greater praise and merit be able to fulfil the will of God in all details of our lives as well as in carrying out the free wishes and orders of His Holiness, to whom we have most willingly offered our all: will, intellect, strength, and the like? [D 4].

Their answer to this question will determine whether or not they become a new religious order. The way they articulate their question may seem strange to us, referring to a vow of obedience rather than expressly to founding an order. However, the text implicitly explains the choice of words by pointing out that they are already vowed to poverty and celibacy. If they also pronounce a vow of obedience to someone within the group, they will become religious.

## Towards a New Methodology

The companions now have a second carefully phrased question. They begin their discernment with the same approach that had led to an easy resolution of the prior question on union: prayer throughout the day followed by sharing in the evenings. But they soon become aware that this second question is proving much more intractable than the first, as the text reveals:

> When we had persisted in prayer and thought for many days without hitting upon any satisfactory resolution of our uncer-

*Personal and Corporate*    87

tainty, we put our hope in the Lord and started to cast about for better ways of working out such a resolution [D 5].

The issue here is one of methodology. They wondered if they could discover how to create a milieu which would make it easier to listen to the voice of the Spirit. Ultimately, it was on that voice that they were relying.

> Our first line of thought went this way: would it expedite our discernment if we all went away to some hermitage for thirty or forty days, giving ourselves over to meditation, fasting and penance, so that God might listen to our desires and mercifully impress on our minds the answer to our question? Or should three or four undertake this enterprise in the name of all with the same intent? Or would it be better if none of us went to the hermitage but all remained in the city, devoting half of every day to this our one principal occupation and the rest of the day to our customary work of preaching and hearing confessions? The half devoted to our principal concern would be the time less crowded with other concerns, more suitable for meditation, reflection and prayer [D 5].

Three practical possibilities are outlined here: (i) that all withdraw from the city and go to a hermitage where they can discern in solitude, (ii) that three or four among them take this course and discern on behalf of the others, (iii) that no one go to a hermitage, but that all remain in the city and continue their discernment. They opt for the third, deciding that all of them will remain in Rome, but with the specification that they give half of each day to their customary pastoral work and the other half to 'meditation, reflection and prayer'. These three proposals show both flexibility and imagination.

## Three Preparations

The companions now agree to put into practice three 'spiritual preparations' that further nuance their methodology.

88 *Towards an Understanding of Ignatian Spirituality*

> The first preparation: each would prepare himself beforehand, would take time for prayer, Masses and meditation in order to strive for joy and peace in the Holy Spirit regarding obedience, labouring as much as he could to have a predilection for obeying rather than commanding, when the consequent glory of God and the praise of his majesty would be equal [D 6].

They are now zooming in on the central issue for discernment: whether to vow obedience to one of themselves. Note especially the call to pray for inner freedom, so that any repugnance a person may feel towards living under obedience will not become a determining criterion in his eventual choice. Such inner freedom will lead to 'joy and peace in the Holy Spirit'.

Now follows another directive that is based on how they understand the working of the Holy Spirit:

> The second preparation: none of the companions would communicate with any other about this matter at issue, or enquire about his reasoning on it. The point of this preparation was to prevent anyone from being persuaded by another and, therefore, biased more toward obedience or the contrary. In this way each would desire as more advantageous only what he derived from his own prayer and meditation [D 6].

Again they are seeking spiritual freedom. They do not want to influence one another while they ponder and pray individually about the issue. Each must reach his conclusion in solitude before God. This insistence on personal prayer being unfettered by the influence of any contemporaneous sharing or discussion is central to their new procedure. We now return to the text:

> The third preparation: each one would think of himself as a stranger to our group who would have no expectation of joining it. Thinking this way he would escape being carried by his emotions more to one opinion and judgement; rather, as if a stranger, he would speak his thought to the group about having or not

having obedience, would by his judgement confirm and recommend what he believed would be for God's greater service, and would make more secure the Society's lasting preservation [D 6].

What at other times is greatly to be desired – a strong sense of belonging to the group – is here acknowledged as a possible obstruction in the discernment. A sense of belonging, with the emotional bonds that it creates, can lead to a distortion of perspective and a lack of inner freedom. Reason and objectivity go out of the window while emotions hold sway.

The companions recognise that they need to distance themselves from their own feelings towards one another so that they may see the issue clearly and objectively. Hence the suggestion that each imagine himself as a stranger to the group, as a benevolent outsider looking in, but with no emotional involvement. The *Spiritual Exercises* describes a similar tactic in presenting the Third Time for making a decision:

> I will imagine a person whom I have never seen or known. Desiring all perfection for that person, I will consider what I would say in order to bring such a one to act and elect for the greater glory of God our Lord and the greater perfection of his or her soul [SE 185].

The companions adjust this tactic to suit the corporate nature of their discernment.

## Pros and Cons, Cons and Pros

They are now ready to turn their attention to the second element in communal discernment, that of sharing the outcome of their prayer. But they have learned the hard way that this sharing needs to be more structured than earlier in their deliberation. Once again they turn to the *Spiritual Exercises*, specifically to the following paragraph:

90 *Towards an Understanding of Ignatian Spirituality*

> I should consider and reason out how many advantages or bene-
> fits accrue to myself from having the office or benefice proposed,
> all of them solely for the praise of God our Lord and the salva-
> tion of my soul; and, on the contrary, I should similarly consider
> the disadvantages and dangers in having it. Then, acting in the
> same manner in the second part, I should consider the advan-
> tages and benefits in not having it, and contrarily the disadvan-
> tages and dangers in not having it [SE 181].

Adapting this teaching to their own current concern, the companions consider the advantages of making a vow of obedience,
then the corresponding disadvantages; after that, the advantages
of not making a vow of obedience, then the corresponding disadvantages. In other words they prepare four lists of reasons. In
reporting back to the group after their individual prayer and reflection, however, they seem to have abridged this protocol. They
simply share the reasons that surfaced against vowing obedience,
and later those that surfaced in its favour. We read:

> With the foregoing spiritual dispositions, we arranged to as-
> semble, all prepared, on the following day. Each one was to
> declare all those disadvantages which could be brought against
> obedience [by vow, to one of our group], all the reasons which
> presented themselves and which anyone of us had found in his
> own private reflection, meditation, and prayer. Each in his turn
> was to make known what he had gathered. For example, one
> said, 'It seems that on account of our failures and sins the words
> "religious" or "obedience" have unseemly connotations among
> the Christian people' [D 7].

Other reasons against vowing obedience and becoming a religious
order follow. They range widely and reveal the ways in which the
companions understood themselves and their vocation, as well as
the civil and ecclesiastical society in which they lived. Having given
a sample of these arguments against obedience the text continues:

*Personal and Corporate*   91

On the next day we argued for the opposite side of the question, each one putting before the group all the advantages and good consequences of such obedience which he had drawn from prayer and meditation; each one took his own turn to present his reflections, sometimes arguing from the impossible situation that would otherwise result, sometimes simply showing the positive values of obedience [D 7].

Again a sample list of such arguments follows. A query is often raised about the companions' decision to present their arguments against obedience first, and only then the arguments in favour. It is not what most people tend to do spontaneously. The companions may sense that some are already leaning towards becoming a religious order, even before the process begins. If so, they may be hoping to provide a reality check by having everyone face the arguments against this course of action first. Acceptance of obedience will not be steamrolled through the assembly.

## Toward Closure

This initial sharing of the reasons against and for obedience that surface in each individual's prayer lays the foundation for the difficult work to follow. The text makes it clear that the companions need a lot of time to work through the complexities of the questions facing them.

During many days, from this side and that, we worked over a mass of data related to the resolution of our problem; we examined and weighed the more forceful and important reasons and took time as usual for prayer, meditation and reflection. By the Lord's help we did at last come to this conclusion, not only with a majority vote but without a single dissenting voice: obedience to somebody among us is highly advantageous and highly necessary in order to accomplish more effectively and exactly our primary desire of fulfilling God's will in all details

92  *Towards an Understanding of Ignatian Spirituality*

of life, in order to preserve the Society more assuredly, and finally in order to provide properly for all the detailed matters of spiritual and temporal business which arise [D 7].

So finally they reach closure. They will found a religious order. They would have been satisfied with a majority decision but in fact they reach consensus. The experience of harmony and joy that accompanies this consensus provides them with what the *Spiritual Exercises* call confirmation.

> When that election or decision has been made, the person who has made it ought with great diligence to go to prayer before God our Lord and to offer him that election, that the Divine Majesty may be pleased to receive and confirm it, if it is conducive to his greater service and praise [SE 183].

The companions are assured that God does accept and approve their decision. The Spirit has been with them. They are now ready to move on to implementation.

The *Deliberation of the First Fathers* is a unique document. This is not to assert that communal discernment had not been part of the Christian tradition before 1539, but there is no other detailed record of such a process as is provided by the *Deliberation*. In recent times it has shown itself to be user-friendly and adaptable to the needs of many groups and organisations, secular as well as religious.

*Part Two*

# Towards
# a Personal Response
# to Ignatian Spirituality

*chapter one*

# Ignatius the Pilgrim

Ignatius Loyola was canonised on 12 March 1622, along with his friend, Francis Xavier, and two other well-known saints, Philip Neri and Teresa of Avila. These four outstanding Christians witnessed to the vibrancy of renewal in the Church of the sixteenth century. They gave expression to the Church's holiness in different and creative ways. Three of the four were born in what is now modern Spain. All lived in a century of great change.

The Renaissance was fostering developments in art and culture, and was transforming approaches to education throughout Europe. The Protestant Reformations – there was more than one – introduced new ideas into theology and spirituality, and challenged the authority of the Roman Church. The voyages of discovery led to a vast expanding of people's imaginative horizons, brought immense wealth back to Europe from recently conquered lands, and opened a new era of missionary work for the Church.

We have learned to pay more attention to the historical context of saints' lives than we may have done in the past. The turbulence of the sixteenth century affected Ignatius's thinking, his choices, his spirituality, and therefore his holiness. He would have been a different person, a different saint, if he had lived in the ninth or nineteenth century.

But under God's providence he walked this earth at a particular time (not any time), in a specific historical era (not some other era), meeting certain people (and not others). It was in these concrete

## 96  *Towards a Personal Response to Ignatian Spirituality*

circumstances that he sought and found God, and that he grew in intimacy with him. We cannot turn Ignatius into a twenty-first century person. We cannot simply imitate him in every aspect of his life. Likewise, knowing historical facts about Ignatius will not of itself contribute much to our own growth. If we want to learn from Ignatius we need to get inside his experience, so far as that is possible. We need to discover how God worked in him.

This need was already expressed very clearly in 1551 by one of Ignatius's friends. Jerome Nadal was one of a number of Jesuits who wanted Ignatius to tell the story of his life. But Nadal wanted it told in a particular way. This is how he reports on his approach to Ignatius: 'I begged the Father to be kind enough to tell us how the Lord had guided him from the beginning of his conversion'. He was not asking for an autobiography in the usual meaning of that word. In standard autobiographies the focus is on the people telling their story, what they did, said, saw, achieved, suffered, and so forth. Ignatius was being asked to recount what God did in him, how God influenced, taught, led, guided, challenged and loved him since his conversion in Loyola in 1521. The focus was to be on God. Readers would learn about God and the ways of God more than about Ignatius and his ways. This was to be the work's importance.

Ignatius was curiously hesitant about telling this story and kept putting off the effort. This was partly due to ill health, partly to the pressure of urgent business, and partly to a lingering fear of vainglory. But perhaps most of all it came from a reticence, quite typical of him, about speaking of his inner experiences of God. However, he eventually dictated an account to another Jesuit, Gonçalves da Câmara, and this relatively short work gives us a precious insight into God's ways of dealing with him. In spite of its not being an autobiography, it is most frequently referred to in English as the *Autobiography*. Other titles, also in use, are perhaps more accurate, such as *A Pilgrim's Journey, Original Testament,* or simply *Reminiscences.*

The first title of this short account was *Acta Patris Ignatii*, and that is the title I will use here when referring to this text.[27] It is one of our main sources for getting inside the experience of Ignatius and learning from it. It can surprise readers who come across this work for the first time that Ignatius narrates his story in the third person. Is this another instance of his reticence? Employing the third person allows him to create a certain distance between himself as narrator and the experiences of God that he is describing. It helps him be more objective. There is also less danger of falling into vainglory – to which he feels vulnerable – if he is not using 'I' and 'me' and 'my' in every other sentence. But most importantly, he gives this third person a name, 'the pilgrim'. In doing this he is offering his readers a key to unlock and enter the narrative.

His story will be about movement, about journeying, about a search, about exploration. God will be seen to accompany him along many paths, now nudging him forward, now restraining him. These paths are, quite literally, the roads of Europe - not forgetting the Mediterranean Sea – that bring him to Montserrat, Manresa, Barcelona, the Holy Land, Alcalá, Salamanca, Paris, Venice and Rome. The pilgrim's paths are also metaphorical or figurative, however, symbolising his inner journey. Over years this will see Ignatius change, develop and grow into the person that God wants him to be.

Neither the starting point of the outer or the inner journeys gives any clue as to where it will end. Convalescing in his family's castle in Loyola, Ignatius can have no idea that the final years of his life will be spent in Rome. The same can be said about his inner journey. This begins with the opening sentence of the *Acta*: 'Up to his twenty-sixth year he was a man given to worldly vanities, and having a vain and overpowering desire to gain renown, he found

---

27. For a fuller discussion of this work and its title see Part I.

98  *Towards a Personal Response to Ignatian Spirituality*

special delight in the exercise of arms' [AIP 1]. The journey ends – at least in the text – at the time of narrating his story when he can say, 'His devotion, that is, his ease in finding God, was always increasing, now more than ever in his entire life. At whatever time or hour he wanted to find God, he found him' [AIP 99]. The *Acta* is mainly the story of that inner journey, of how God led him from being an ambitious, boisterous knight, filled with dreams of chivalry, to becoming a person whose only desire was 'to praise, reverence and serve God our Lord'.

All Christians are pilgrims. We are on a journey, like Abraham who 'set out, not knowing where he was going' (Heb 11:8). Abraham is praised for his faith, which in this context is synonymous with trust. He trusted the God who had called him. He did not need to know the destination. It was enough that God was with him. So too with Ignatius, who trusted that God would not desert him, abandon him, or allow him to go too far astray. Both his story and that of Abraham invite us to a similar trust. Life will always bring changes, gains and losses, clarity and confusion. Through it all we are encouraged to leave ourselves in the hands of God, to allow him to write our own personal story.

### *Prayer Suggestion*

The Lord your God, who goes before you, is the one who will fight for you, just as he did for you in Egypt before your very eyes, and in the wilderness, where you saw how the Lord your God carried you, just as one carries a child, all the way that you travelled until you reached this place.

(Deut 1:30-31)

*chapter two*

# Learning from Daydreams

The early part of Ignatius's life is probably better known than his last years in Rome. He was wounded while leading the defence of the citadel of Pamplona against an invading French army. That stubborn, heroic but futile display of bravery remains readily in the memory. Similarly the scene where he lay on his bed in the castle of Loyola, recovering from his wounds and subsequent surgery, also captures the imagination. We may well have gone through periods of convalescence ourselves and so can empathise with the boredom he felt.

Ignatius did not have a radio at his side or a television monitor facing his bed or a smartphone in his hand. He tried to relieve the tedium – and the pain – by asking for what most appealed to his taste in reading, romances of chivalry. But none could be found in the castle; it was apparently not a household where much reading was done. All that came to hand was a book of Lives of the Saints, and the *Life of Christ* by a medieval Carthusian, Ludolph of Saxony.

What took place in Ignatius during those months of recovery at Loyola is often called his conversion. It might be more correct to see it as the beginning of his conversion. This was to be a gradual process, continuing through his later experiences at Manresa and beyond. The word 'conversion' itself can be misleading if interpreted too narrowly, as it often is, to refer exclusively to moral behaviour. Morality is only one dimension of conversion, and

100    *Towards a Personal Response to Ignatian Spirituality*

perhaps not the most profound. Underlying it there is a more radical transformation: a conversion or a turning to God.

Having made that 'turn' a person sees everything in a new way. Remember that Native American saying, 'Where you plant your feet determines what you see'. The person who has turned to God now has a new and more expansive horizon. Beauty reveals itself in unexpected places. Other people are more appreciated and easier to love. Virtue becomes attractive. Personal priorities begin to be revised. New decisions are called for and made.

This is the process that began for Ignatius as he convalesced. It was, of course, the grace of God at work. But what way did grace 'get through' to Ignatius? We tend, perhaps, to think of God speaking to our reason, our understanding or our conscience, or drawing us through our feelings. Both reason and feelings surely came to be involved in Ignatius's conversion, but it all started off with his imagination, his ability to daydream.

The lack of books telling stories of knights and ladies, thrilling adventures and great deeds, loyalty to a king and love of a fair maiden, did not prevent Ignatius from imagining such scenarios. This was the imaginative world in which he normally lived. Of course, he was always the hero! He tells us in the *Acta* that he spent many hours in such daydreams, and in one in particular:

> He dreamed what he would achieve in the service of a certain lady and thought of the means he would take to go to the land where she lived, the clever sayings and words he would speak to her, and the knightly deeds he would perform for her. He was so enraptured with these thoughts of his that he never considered how impossible it was for him to accomplish them [AIP 6].

When Ignatius turned to the *Life of Christ* and the Lives of the Saints his vivid imagination was still at play. He asked himself, 'What if I were to do what St Francis did, or to do what St Dominic did?'

*Learning from Daydreams* 101

He was daydreaming, playing in his imagination with an alternative set of possibilities to those of being the chivalrous knight. Yet he was still thinking like a knight. He was focusing not on the inner life of Christ and the saints, not on the values they lived by, but on their great and heroic deeds. Soon the speculative question ('What if I were. . .?') became an imperative: 'St Dominic did this, so I have to do it too. St Francis did this, so I have to do it too' [7]. It was an impulsive, immature response, of no great spiritual depth. Yet it was enough to allow God to enter the door that was opening and to enlighten Ignatius further.

Like many energetic people who have been forced into inactivity by illness, Ignatius was becoming more reflective. He was growing more attentive to everything that he was experiencing. More importantly, however, he was starting to question the changes of mood caused by his reading and his daydreaming. Imagining himself as the romantic, swashbuckling knight brought him great delight, but so did imagining himself performing great deeds for God, mostly by imitating the penitential practices of the saints. He really enjoyed playing the hero!

But now he began to notice a difference in the *aftermath* of the two kinds of daydreaming. Whenever he stopped musing about knightly honour and adventure 'he found that he was dry and unhappy'. But whenever he had been engaged with thoughts about the great deeds he would do for God, 'even after they had left him he remained happy and joyful'. Noticing all this did not immediately bring understanding,

> until one day his eyes were partially opened and he began to wonder at this difference and to reflect upon it . . . and little by little he came to perceive the different spirits that were moving him: one coming from the devil, the other coming from God [AIP 8].

The word 'spirit' in this context can be puzzling for some people today. It relates to movements within us, sometimes accompanied

102  *Towards a Personal Response to Ignatian Spirituality*

by a lot of emotion, that influence us in some way. We find ourselves drawn towards some person or idea or a course of action. This brings with it feelings of enthusiasm, elation, desire, love, and so on. Or we find ourselves repelled by some person, idea, or course of action. This, on the contrary, brings with it feelings of distaste, revulsion, fear, antagonism, and so forth.

When we notice what is going on, there are two questions we can ask. The first is: where is this spirit, this movement, leading me? If I follow the direction of this movement and let it carry me along, will I find myself coming nearer to God? Or will I be wandering away from God? The second question is: where has this spirit, this movement, come from? Has it come from God or from some source that is not God – which Ignatius calls the devil? The two questions are interlinked. A movement that is bringing me towards God is evidently one that has come from God. Whereas a movement that is leading me away from God is obviously coming from a source other than God.

This was, in fairly straightforward terms, what Ignatius learned at Loyola. It was the first step in his understanding of *discernment*. This theological word, sometimes overused or misunderstood nowadays, refers to the art of distinguishing one kind of spirit or movement from another. Discernment is at the heart of what we now call Ignatian spirituality. As with Ignatius it begins with awareness, with noticing, with paying attention to all our inner experiences. Then come the questioning and the interpretation. Ultimately we are asking 'Where is God in all of this?' 'How is God communicating with me here?' We do not need extraordinary experiences in order to discern. God speaks through our quite mundane human experiences of mind, heart and imagination. All that is required on our side is attentiveness and prayerful reflection. You could begin, as Ignatius did, with the help of your own daydreams!

### Prayer Suggestion

Beloved, do not believe every spirit, but test the spirits to see whether they are from God; for many false prophets have gone out into the world. By this you know the Spirit of God: every spirit that confesses that Jesus Christ has come in the flesh is from God, and every spirit that does not confess Jesus is not from God.

(1 Jn 4:1-3).

*chapter three*

# Three Things I Pray

The seventies' hit musical *Godspell* presented the story of Jesus in an upbeat, contemporary idiom. This resonated with a whole generation, many of whom, although nominally Christian, had drifted away from organised religion. One of the show's best-loved songs was the infectious 'Day by Day'. Not many people know that this song was based on a prayer by a medieval English bishop, St Richard of Chichester (1197-1253). In its original and fuller form it reads:

> Thanks be to you, my Lord Jesus Christ,
> for all the benefits you have given me,
> for all the pains and insults you have borne for me.
> O most merciful Redeemer, Friend, and Brother,
> may I know you more clearly,
> love you more dearly,
> follow you more nearly,
> day by day. Amen.

As audiences at *Godspell* swayed to the rhythm and sang along with the music, they were often being drawn into a spiritual experience. They were getting in touch with some of their deepest desires. As they expressed in words and music their, perhaps unconscious, yearning for a close relationship with Jesus – 'Three things I pray' – the religious dimension of their lives was being revived, stirred into new life.

Was Ignatius familiar with this prayer of Richard of Chichester? We do not know. But whether he was or not, he certainly came close to duplicating its final lines in the *Spiritual Exercises*. In introducing the kind of prayer that we know today as gospel, or Ignatian, contemplation, he writes, 'The third prelude will be to ask for what I desire. Here it will be to ask for an interior knowledge of Our Lord, who became human for me, that I may love him more intensely and follow him more closely' [SE 104]. The wording is more sober, and it lacks the rhyme and rhythm of Richard's prayer or the *Godspel* song, but the 'three things I pray' are essentially the same: to know, to love and to follow Christ. Moreover, Ignatius has added a clarifying word of great importance, the adjective 'interior', to describe the knowledge of Christ that is desired. We will need to return to this.

Ignatius's approach to gospel contemplation is a version of *lectio divina,* the venerable monastic way of prayer that has spread well beyond monastic circles in our day. What is characteristic of the Ignatian approach, however, is the stress on the use of the imagination. He suggests an imaginative entering into a gospel scene or event – what the tradition calls a 'mystery' – in Christ's life, so that we become totally immersed in it. We gaze at the persons, listen to what they are saying, observe what they are doing. We speak with Jesus or with some other person or persons in the scene about what is happening and what reactions this is evoking in us. We might even 'take part' in the scene, for example, having our feet washed by Jesus at the Last Supper, or helping to place the body of Jesus in the tomb. We can do this either by remaining ourselves, or by imaginatively becoming one of the gospel characters, for example Peter or Mary of Magdala, or by imaginatively becoming an 'extra', for example, another blind beggar in a scene of healing. There is no one way of becoming part of a gospel event; whatever way works for us is best.

All of this is aimed at inserting ourselves deeply into the 'mystery' we are contemplating. It is a way of ensuring that the knowledge of Christ that we are asking for will be truly 'interior'. What

# 106 *Towards a Personal Response to Ignatian Spirituality*

then is meant by interior knowledge? We might explain what we mean by contrasting such interior, or intimate, knowledge of a person with a knowledge that is objective, intellectual, scholarly or clinical. We are touching here on the difference between *knowing* a person and *knowing about* a person. The latter can be attained through gathering facts and processing information. It is the result of research and study. In gospel contemplation, however, we are seeking the kind of knowledge that a wife may have of her husband, or a father of his child, or a lover of her beloved.

Such knowledge only comes from two people being together over a period of time, perhaps many years, interacting with each other, sharing life's experiences, loving each other. Accordingly, in gospel contemplation we remain present to Jesus as he is born, grows, relates, works, travels, teaches, rejoices, suffers, and so forth. We want to get inside his experience, not just to know the external details of his life. We desire *to know him from the inside out.* Such intimate knowledge of another person can never be forced but is always pure gift. Hence we need to keep asking Jesus to be gracious and to reveal himself. '"Come", my heart says, "seek his face!" Your face, Lord, do I seek. Do not hide your face from me' (Ps 27:8-9). Living with this desire, we develop a contemplative attitude towards Christ. We are willing to wait patiently, allowing him to reveal himself as he really is, and not as we might want him to be.

Ignatius had first learned about this kind of prayer from Ludolph of Saxony's *Life of Christ*, which he had read during his convalescence in Loyola. In the preface to this work the author writes about entering gospel scenes or events:

> Hear and see these things being narrated, as though you were hearing with your own ears and seeing with your own eyes, for these things are most sweet to him who thinks on them with desire, and even more so to him who tastes them. And though many of these are narrated as past events, you must meditate them all as though they were happening in the present moment, because in this way you will certainly taste a greater sweetness.

Read then of what has been done as though they were happening now. Bring before your eyes past actions as though they were present. Then you will feel how full of wisdom and delight they are.

All relationships that have any depth involve mutuality. As we desire that Jesus reveal himself to us, so too we reveal ourselves to Jesus. We share with him our own lives, our struggles and successes, the darkness of our doubts and the brightness of our hopes. We allow him to get to know us, to have an interior knowledge of us, at the same time as we receive an interior knowledge of him. Our human need *to be known* by the other - or the divine Other – lies very deeply within us. It complements our desire to know the other, or the divine Other. This mutuality brings a wholeness to the loving relationship that we long for with God in Christ. As Ignatius wrote towards the end of the *Spiritual Exercises*:

> Love consists in a mutual communication between the two persons. That is, the one who loves gives and communicates to the beloved what he or she has, or a part of what the person has or can have; and the beloved in return does the same to the lover . . . Each shares with the other [SE 231].

### *Prayer Suggestion*

> I regard everything as loss because of the surpassing value of knowing Christ Jesus my Lord . . . I want to know Christ and the power of his resurrection and the sharing of his sufferings by becoming like him in his death, if somehow I may attain the resurrection from the dead.
>
> (Phil 3:8, 10-11)

*chapter four*

# Light and Darkness

People who have undergone a deep conversion, whether moral or spiritual, or both, tend initially to experience a period of unruffled consolation. To friends and observers it may even seem that they are 'on a high'. This is what happened to Ignatius at the beginning of his stay in Manresa. In the *Acta* he says, 'Up to this time he continued undisturbed in the same interior state of great and constant joy without knowing anything about internal spiritual matters' [AIP 20]. As he looks back he realises that the joy or consolation of that period of his life was accompanied by much ignorance. He is not referring to ignorance of book-learning but to lack of experience of the inner life. Such experience was not long in coming.

The first disturbance that shook his composure was a temptation to discouragement, an agitated questioning of his ability to persevere in his good intentions. 'Perceiving that this was the voice of the enemy, he likewise interiorly answered and with great courage: "O, you wretch! Can you promise me one hour of life?" Thus he overcame the temptation and remained tranquil' [AIP 20]. However, dealing well with this experience of inner turmoil was only the beginning. Ignatius continues his story:

> After the above-mentioned temptation, he began to feel notable changes in his soul. Sometimes he was so dejected that he found no enjoyment in the prayers he recited, not even in attending

*Light and Darkness* 109

Mass, nor in any other form of prayer. Sometimes the exact opposite happened to him, and so suddenly that it seemed he had stripped away all sadness and desolation, just as one strips a cloak from another's shoulder. He was astonished at these changes, which he had never before experienced, and said to himself: 'What kind of a new life is this that we are now beginning?' [AIP 21].

Does any of this seem familiar? Have you noticed in your own life a similar pattern of alternating moods in the context of your beliefs or commitments? Have you undergone similar shifts of feeling in relation to your faith in God, or to your efforts to pray, or to attending Mass – elation and deflation, warmth and coldness, comfort and boredom? If so, have you too reacted with surprise, bewilderment, confusion? What Ignatius is describing, and what many good people also experience, is quite normal. At the time the new convert did not know this. In his ignorance Ignatius thought that he should always be joyful or in consolation, always 'on a high'. Simply turn to God, pray, do penance, lead a good life, and you will continually be at peace. Not so!

My child, when you come to serve the Lord, prepare yourself for testing. Set your heart right and be steadfast, and do not be impetuous in time of calamity (Sir 2:1-2).

Being *impetuous* would involve surrendering to the natural urge to give up when we are getting no satisfaction from our religious practice. Being *steadfast* involves the opposite: continuing to trust God, to pray and go to Mass in spite of the aridity, boredom, darkness or even pain of the experience. Ignatius tends to use the word 'desolation' to cover all kinds of emotional disturbance, or the absence of any emotional response at all, in our relationship with God. Having learned from his own experience, however, he does not see desolation in wholly negative terms, as though it were a spiritual catastrophe. He urges us to remain faithful, to refuse to give in to the desolation, and to rely on God to lead us out of

110   *Towards a Personal Response to Ignatian Spirituality*

the quagmire in his own time. If we take that approach, desolation can become an opportunity for an increase in self-knowledge, a purifying of our motives, and growth in our love of God.

In the *Spiritual Exercises*, Ignatius wrote in the Rules for the Discernment of Spirits: 'When we are in desolation we should think that the Lord has left us to our own powers in order to test us' – see the quotation from Sirach above – 'so that we may prove ourselves by resisting the various agitations and temptations of the enemy' [SE 320]. We see here how the mature Ignatius, in contrast to the immature convert of his early days at Manresa, has come to understand the nature of desolation and is no longer surprised or frightened by it. It is simply a normal episode in the spiritual life, to be dealt with firmly, and indeed as calmly as we are able.

At the heart of all desolation there lies a sense that God is either distant or wholly absent; that God has withdrawn his love from us and abandoned us. This is often accompanied by a reactive tendency on our part to blame ourselves for what is happening. Why would God be treating us like this unless we had done something wrong? It must be our fault! God must be punishing us! Such thoughts are almost always untrue as well as unhelpful, and need to be resolutely set aside. Otherwise we get sucked even deeper into the desolation, into our feelings of isolation, abandonment, helplessness and self-recrimination.

For this reason, what follows in the above quotation from Ignatius's Rules is so important: 'For we can do this [i.e. resist the desolation] with God's help, which always remains available, even if we do not clearly perceive it' [SE 320]. Another way of expressing this teaching is that a *felt* absence of God is not the same as a *real* absence. We may not *feel* that God is with us but that does not mean that God is *really* not with us. Indeed, faith assures us that God is always present to us, even if, in desolation, it is a faith that cannot see, that is forced to live in darkness. Although spoken in a different context, the words of Jesus to doubting Thomas may offer encouragement: 'Blessed are those who have not seen and yet have come to believe' (Jn 20:29).

*Light and Darkness* 111

We experience a great freedom once we come to accept that it is quite normal for periods of desolation to alternate with periods of consolation, when we feel comfort, joy and ease in our relationship with God. We are no longer overly dependent on the state of our feelings. Our faith has stronger, deeper roots. We learn to pray with as much confidence out of sadness, gloom and spiritual dryness as out of joy, lightness of heart and bubbling enthusiasm. Ignatius and the wider Christian tradition assure us that when darkness comes, either from within ourselves or from devastating events in our lives, we can still cling in faith to the Lord's words:

> Can a woman forget her nursing child?
> Or show no compassion for the child of her womb?
> Even these may forget,
> yet I will not forget you (Is 49:15).

Consequently, we can be as content to pray like Jacob wrestling all night with the angel (Gen 32:22-32) as like Mary, the sister of Martha, who sat quietly at Jesus' feet listening to him speak (Lk 10:38-42). One mode of prayer is not better than the other.

The pattern of alternating moods that Ignatius experienced at Manresa opened up for him the reality of a 'new life'. Such a development in ourselves is to be welcomed, not avoided, because through it God will lead us more fully into his own divine life.

## *Prayer Suggestion*

Out of the depths I cry to you, O Lord.
Lord, hear my voice!
Let your ears be attentive to the voice of
my supplications!
I wait for the Lord, my soul waits,
and in his word I hope;
my soul waits for the Lord
more than those who watch for the morning,
O Israel, hope in the Lord!
For with the Lord there is steadfast love,
and with him is great power to redeem.

(Ps 130:1-2, 5-7)

*chapter five*

# Freedom for Discernment

Life would be simpler, less hassled and more serene, if only we did not have so many decisions to make! True, but might that life be somehow less than fully human? God seems to have created us to be decision-makers. 'I have set before you life and death, blessings and curses. Choose life so that you and your descendants may live' (Deut 30:19).

The Spiritual Exercises offers a way of coming to a good decision on a major issue in a person's life. For example, a person may be facing a choice about getting married, or entering religious life, or studying for a degree, or changing career or volunteering for development work overseas. These are difficult decisions, not to be taken lightly. They will affect many people besides the one making the choice. A Christian will want to make such a decision in line with Christ's teaching and example, or in other words by using the criteria of gospel values. More bluntly, a Christian will not simply be asking 'What do *I* want to do?' but 'What does *God* want me to do?' A believer will want to say with conviction, as Jesus did, 'My food is to do the will of him who sent me, and to complete his work' (Jn 4:34).

The question about what God wants of me can be experienced as oppressive and threatening unless I know in my heart and in my gut that God loves me unconditionally. 'Because you are precious in my sight, and honoured, and I love you' (Is 43:4). The Christian God is personal, relational, close at hand and involved

114  *Towards a Personal Response to Ignatian Spirituality*

in my life. He loves me and wants what is best for me. 'For surely I know the plans I have for you, says the Lord, plans for your welfare and not for harm, to give you a future with hope' (Jer 29:11). Do I hear these encouraging words as addressed to me 'by name'? What resonance do they have within me? Do these words leave me cold and apathetic or do they stir and warm my heart?

If such words do offer me an assurance that the God who loves me will be with me, then I can proceed with confidence towards my decision. Indeed, God and I will be making this decision together! Even further, I will know that what God wants of me is not only for my good, but that it will turn out to coincide with my own deepest desires. There need be no clash between what *I* want and what *God* wants!

Yet, even with such assurance, decision-making is often a difficult process, marked by unsettling fluctuations of mood, and even by painful inner struggle. Why might this be? It is because once I begin to face the prospect of a major turning point in my life, one that will require a radical change and a deep personal commitment, all kinds of feelings begin to surface. Some of these will carry me along happily enough, such as attraction, energy, generosity, enthusiasm and hope. But others will disturb me and hold me back, such as anxiety, fear, lethargy, self-doubt and anger.

How I deal with these fluctuations, this emotional roller coaster, is at the core of what is called discernment. All such feelings, invigorating or enervating, uplifting or depressing, can bring valuable self-knowledge, which is crucial in discernment. But more importantly, when interpreted wisely, these feelings can also reveal the direction in which God is leading me.

There is yet another dimension to this experience. By acknowledging and facing these conflicting feelings I am enabled *to grow in freedom*. The freedom in question here is not the kind that safeguards me from outside pressures or coercion, such as political freedom or freedom of worship or freedom of speech. It is an *inner* freedom, a *spiritual* freedom. This allows me to see myself and the world around me with a certain detachment, without my vision being blurred or distorted by my passions. Spiritual freedom

*Freedom for Discernment* 115

also enables me to respond with authenticity and generosity to whatever surfaces in my reasoning and in my affectivity. I am no longer hindered or manipulated by un-freedoms within me.

Much of the Spiritual Exercises revolves around this issue of spiritual freedom, suggesting ways of opening myself to it and attaining it under God's grace. In the earlier parts of the Exercises the emphasis is more on a *freedom from* sin, the roots of sin, inner disorder, addictions, obsessions, selfishness, apathy, and the baleful influence of those cultural values that are opposed to the Gospel. But soon the emphasis shifts to a *freedom for* discipleship, witness, service, ministry, loving relationships, self-emptying – whatever it is that God is asking of me. Freedom exists on different levels of the human psyche, and I may well need patience as I am being guided through these levels. The ultimate test of my freedom lies in one question: do I want *only* what God wants? There is no freedom greater than being able to give a positive 'yes!' to this challenging question. Mostly, we find ourselves 'on our way' to such an answer.

The difficulty that I have in making key decisions in my life can be caused by many factors. Sometimes it is due to the sheer complexity of my life situation; at others it may be due to the number of imponderables that face me as I look to the future. At times the problem is that the options that are opening up for me all appear equally attractive, worthy and full of promise. Again, it may seem that God is absent or silent or uncaring, and not supplying me with any guidance whatsoever. In numerous cases the difficulty is simply that I do not have sufficient inner freedom to make a good decision.

It may not be immediately apparent that this is the block that I am experiencing. I may not be conscious of what is really going on within me. Lack of inner freedom often has a way of concealing itself like a chameleon. But when my lack of freedom becomes undeniable, then I will need to concentrate my desires and prayer on asking God to set me free.

Once my prayer is heard, it is surprising how many other things may fall into place. Where matters formerly seemed confused,

116 *Towards a Personal Response to Ignatian Spirituality*

they are now remarkably clear; where I once felt trapped in debilitating laziness, I now feel energised; where I was full of fear, I am now ready to make my decision with courage.

Against this background it is interesting to read how Ignatius described his *Spiritual Exercises*:

> Any means of preparing and disposing our soul to rid itself of all its disordered affections and then, after their removal, of seeking and finding God's will in the ordering of our life for the salvation of our soul [SE 1].

And in another paragraph:

> Spiritual Exercises to overcome oneself and to order one's life, without reaching a decision through some disordered affection [SE 21].

The language and tone are those of a sixteenth-century writer, and may not spontaneously appeal to a twenty-first century reader. Yet the content, the substance of Ignatius's words speaks persuasively to our contemporary experience. We know this because the Spiritual Exercises continue to offer many people throughout the world a way forward in the life of the spirit. They have never been more in demand. These Exercises continue to help us grow into freedom as mature Christian disciples, and to use this freedom in the service of God and of God's people.

### *Prayer Suggestion*

> You were called to freedom, brothers and sisters;
> only do not use your freedom as an opportunity for
> self-indulgence, but through love become slaves
> to one another.

(Gal 5:13)

*chapter six*

# To the Greater Glory

Look at the façade of any Jesuit church, or gaze around its interior, and you will almost certainly find the inscription AMDG. You will also find it on many buildings used for Jesuit ministries, such as schools and retreat houses, as well as on books, magazines, letterheads and so on. AMDG stands for the Latin words '*ad maiorem Dei gloriam*', or in English 'To the greater glory of God'. This phrase is often considered to be the Jesuit motto or maxim. It was a favourite expression of Ignatius.

Glory is an extremely rich and multi-layered concept, one that is laden with mystery. In the Bible the phrase 'the glory of God' can be a synonym for God himself. In particular, it points to a manifestation of God's presence that makes it almost palpable. In Ezekiel the glory of God is said to leave Jerusalem (Ez 10) or to return to the Temple (Ez 43). While humans can never see the Godhead, they may behold his glory when it appears. This understanding is also associated with the pillar of cloud by day and the pillar of fire by night during the journey of the Israelites across the desert (Ex 13:21-22). It may also refer to a more everyday occurrence: 'The heavens are telling the glory of God' (Ps 19:1).

When we speak of our giving glory to God, we are using the term in a somewhat different but related way. Glory is not something that God lacks, so that we can give it to him. If God were to be deficient in anything he would not be God! It may help to underline two central aspects of 'giving glory'. First, it is a recognition

118 *Towards a Personal Response to Ignatian Spirituality*

and acknowledgement of the supreme greatness of God, and then it is a desire and need to praise him for his greatness. In Common Preface IV of the Mass we pray:

> For, although you have no need of our praise,
> yet our thanksgiving is itself your gift,
> since our praises add nothing to your greatness
> but profit us for salvation.

This is close to saying, 'You have no need that we should give you glory, yet our longing to give you glory is itself your gift'. Remember that we can acknowledge and praise God's greatness only because he makes it possible for us to do so. It is not God's need but ours that is at issue here.

Giving God glory has to do with us – with our faith, our sense of the transcendent, our inner attitudes and our feelings towards God. It has to do with our sense of the mystery of the divine. Are we in touch with all that this implies? Or is our God too small? When we say 'Glory be to the Father, and to the Son, and to the Holy Spirit', are our emotions in harmony with our words? When we sing 'Glory to God in the highest', are our spirits lifted through this joyful proclamation?

Do we recognise in 'glory' a word that embraces our sentiments of reverence, adoration, wonder, awe and creaturehood? Does it signify our gratitude and release our desire to praise? Or do we say the word – even in prayer – without any feeling? Has the word 'glory' become meaningless? Has the salt lost its taste? We may have something to learn from Pentecostal churches where giving God glory is vibrant, even exuberant, and central to their worship.

In 1609 a young woman of twenty-four was arranging her hair before a mirror in her lodgings near St Clement's Churchyard on The Strand in London when she had an extraordinary experience. For many years Mary Ward had been trying to discover how God wanted her to live her life. In this mystical experience, which came unexpectedly in the course of a mundane activity, God showed her that her current plans to enter the Carmelite Order were not what he desired,

> but some other thing was determined for me, without all comparison more to the glory of God . . . I did not see what the assured good thing would be, but the glory of God which was to come through it, showed itself inexplicably and so abundantly as to fill my soul in such a way that I remained for a good space without feeling or hearing anything but the sound 'GLORY, GLORY, GLORY' (Autobiography).

Here God is promising Mary that he has another call, another gift in mind for her. This as yet unnamed vocation will give God greater glory than would her entry into Carmel. As this promise is being given she is taken out of herself, and so filled with God, that the word 'GLORY' in all its intensity resonates at the depth of her being. Like Abraham she is being empowered to 'set out, not knowing where she was going' (Heb 11:8). Later, after further enlightenment, she was to found an Ignatian congregation for women; its two branches are known today as the Congregation of Jesus (CJ) and the Institute of the Blessed Virgin Mary (IBVM/ Loreto).

Already, Mary Ward had something of the Ignatian spirit through her desire to give herself to what was 'without comparison *more* to the glory of God'. The AMDG motto is not just about glory but *greater* glory. Ignatius frequently uses this comparative form of speech. It is an expression of his magnanimity, his chivalric spirit, never satisfied with the good but always seeking the better. In the *Spiritual Exercises* he writes: 'We ought to desire and choose only that which is *more* conducive to the end for which we are created' [SE 23]. Later, in the *Constitutions* when laying down the criteria by which Jesuits are to choose which ministries to undertake, he insists:

> One should keep the greater service of God and the more universal good before his eyes . . . That part of the vineyard ought

120　*Towards a Personal Response to Ignatian Spirituality*

to be chosen which has greater need . . . where the greater fruit will probably be reaped [C 622].

This habitual way of thinking in comparative terms, of desiring God's *greater* service and *greater* glory, will always draw us beyond where we are now. It is never an easy or convenient course to follow but it can bring the best out of us. It invites us to be willing to leave our comfort zone, to be challenged and stretched by new possibilities and fresh horizons. It brings Ignatian people to the frontiers of evangelisation.

In these reflections we have taken two approaches to the motto AMDG. The first raised questions about the feelings that accompany our use of the word 'glory' in worship and prayer. I suspect that the feelings that would spontaneously call forth a cry of 'Glory to God!' in Ignatius and Mary Ward came more spontaneously to them than they do to us. This has something to do with the way our images of God have changed. In earlier times the holiness, majesty, awesomeness and otherness of God were more evident to believers and touched them more deeply. In our day we have a diminished sensibility to these transcendent qualities in God. This is our loss. We might even say that we have domesticated God!

Our second approach recognised that giving glory to God is not only a matter of feelings and of words. Again in the *Spiritual Exercises* Ignatius teaches that 'Love ought to manifest itself more by deeds than by words' [SE 230]. We can say the same about giving God glory. For Ignatius doing good, being of service to others, helping wherever we can, being committed to justice – all this gives glory to God. His is a spirituality of active involvement in our world. We are encouraged to be 'people for others'. It is easy to see why the words 'glory' and 'service' are almost synonyms for Ignatius. The greater service *is* the greater glory; the greater glory *is* the greater service. God is glorified in any service we give to the Church and to other people. Such activity acknowledges God's existence and manifests God's presence.

We might encourage one another by offering the blessing that Ignatius wrote at the end of one of his letters: 'May you always persevere, growing in God's service, with much honour and glory to him and great benefit to his holy Church.'

### *Prayer Suggestion*

You are worthy, our Lord and God,
to receive glory and honour and power,
for you created all things
and by your will they existed and were created.

(Rev 4:11)

*chapter seven*

# The Call to Interiority

One of the most inspiring spiritual writers of recent times was the Jesuit, Cardinal Carlo Maria Martini, who died in 2012. A respected scripture scholar, he served for more than twenty years as Archbishop of Milan. He then retired to a life of prayer and study in Jerusalem. During his retirement he wrote an article in the course of which he asked what message St Ignatius might have for the third millennium. This seems a good question to pose in the final chapter of this book as well. The core of Martini's answer is as follows:

> I think there is one especially salient message Ignatius can give us: the great value of interiority. I mean by this everything that has to do with the sphere of the heart, of deep intentionality, of decisions made from within.

Interiority is precisely the word that I too would use. Self-knowledge, purifying the heart, the inner journey, finding one's centre, the still point – these and other similar ideas and images have constantly appeared in the Christian spiritual tradition. They echo but go beyond the older Greek philosophical teaching attributed to Socrates, 'The unreflected life is not worth living'. In the Christian experience all of this is linked with prayer – not just saying prayers but praying unceasingly, really becoming people of prayer. One might even paraphrase Socrates and say, 'The prayer-less life is not worth living'.

The argument for interiority today is not simply that it has been a continuous part of the Christian spiritual tradition. It is also that interiority is the antidote to much that is insidiously destructive in our contemporary society. The secularisation of culture, the frantic pace of life, the pressures of competition, the seductiveness of consumerism, the mind-controlling influence of both social and mass media, the intrusiveness of advertising – these and other influences mould our way of living. Busyness replaces reflectiveness, anxiety replaces contentment, and the craving for instant gratification replaces thoughtful attention to long-term goals. Even the quality of our most precious relationships is frequently put at risk. We are drawn to live superficially, on the surface of things, losing touch with our deeper and more authentic selves.

We may not individually have succumbed to all these dangers, yet few would deny experiencing a struggle to 'live out of our centre' and to act in accordance with our highest ideals and deepest desires. These desires may even remain hidden or buried, lost from consciousness. 'What do you *really* want?' is often a surprisingly difficult question for people to answer spontaneously and with conviction.

We may also be deceived by the apparent good. Take the example of hyper-activism. Some people go from one good deed to another, always on the move, always involved in some activity. They never pause and reflect; they never put time aside simply to be by themselves, enjoying the beauties of God's creation, or the uplifting sounds of great music, or the pleasures of reading a well-written book. Their activity has become compulsive. It is no longer freely chosen. They would not know what to do if they stopped. In fact they are terrified of being still, and maybe even more of silence. Solitude would be a kind of hell!

Ignatius was convinced that good people are not likely to be deceived or led astray by blatant or gross temptations. Instead they have to be lured by a suggestion that either *appears* to be good, or really *is* good but not appropriate at this particular time. He writes in the *Spiritual Exercises*:

124 *Towards a Personal Response to Ignatian Spirituality*

> It is characteristic of the evil angel, who takes on the appearance
> of an angel of light, to enter by going along the same way as
> the devout soul, and then to exit by his own way with success
> for himself. That is, he brings good and holy thoughts attractive
> to such an upright soul and then strives little by little to get his
> own way, by enticing the soul over to his own hidden deceits
> and evil intentions [SE 332].

This quotation from the 'Rules for Discernment' addresses a
situation where the temptation itself, and the best ways of dealing
with it, are both extremely subtle. The underlying presupposition
is clear, however. We recognise the temptation for what it is, we
discover what is really happening, *only if we are exercising interiority*. Without self-awareness, and a sensitivity to how God and the
evil spirit are working in us, we will be deceived. In our example,
we will be drawn into a compulsive activism because it *seems* to
be good – unless we can reflect, enter our inner space where God
speaks, and learn what God really wants of us at this time. It may
be to act, or it may be not to act. But in either case prayerful reflectiveness will lead to a genuinely free decision on our part.

The practice that Ignatius proposes to help us grow in interiority is the Consciousness Examen. An older generation knew this
as the Examination of Conscience, where we looked back on the
day – or some other period of time – and sought to discover where
and how we had sinned and offended God. This led to an expression of sorrow or regret, followed by a purpose of amendment.
This exercise served many people well. However, a closer look at
what is found in the *Spiritual Exercises* reveals a more expansive
approach. The shift from the word 'conscience' to 'consciousness'
is the key that allows us to see the difference.

Conscience is the moral sense that we possess that enables us
to distinguish right from wrong. The Examination of Conscience
tended to focus on sin and the occasions of sin, on failure to obey
the law of God, and on our need to be forgiven. This is not left
aside in the Consciousness Examen but it becomes part of some-

thing bigger and more positive. Focusing on consciousness opens up the many ways in which we can become sensitive to the presence or absence of God in our lives. As we allow the day – or whatever period of time we are 'examining' – to pass before our inner eyes, we try to become aware of the situations, the events, the people where we found God, and those other situations, events and people where it was difficult to find him. We can pause in thanksgiving when God's presence was palpable, and pause in sorrow when we missed, ignored or did not appreciate that presence.

In activating our conscience, we mainly make use of our powers of reasoning, enlightened by faith. Consciousness, however, allows us to explore the whole area of affectivity, our inner world of feelings and emotions, including the world of our imagination. We learn to notice our changing moods and other subjective movements, the images that surface – whether they attract or repel us – and to take this inner world seriously. In time we discover how rich this world is and, through discernment, how God is present and active in the mix.

The examination of conscience has a slightly different emphasis. Since it deals primarily with sin and the occasions of sin, most attention is given to actions that are freely carried out. Consciousness, on the other hand, includes a range of spontaneous, 'non-free' movements, emotional reactions over which we have no control. This is part of the messiness of life. But God is as much in this swirling, unpredictable mingling of spontaneities as in our most rational thinking. Once we recognise this, we are on the way to discerning and interpreting how God is leading us and guiding our lives. The whole adventure begins when we answer the call to interiority.

## *Prayer Suggestion*

A new heart I will give you, and a new spirit I will put within you; and I will remove from your body the heart of stone and give you a heart of flesh. I will put my spirit within you, and make you follow my statutes and be careful to observe my ordinances.

(Ez 36:26-27)